Gourmet MUSTARDS

The How-Tos of Making & Cooking with Mustards

Helene Sawyer and Cheryl Long

Previously published by Culinary Arts Ltd
Now Revised and Expanded

SIBYL
PUBLICATIONS
Portland, Oregon

Published by SIBYL Publications, Inc. • 1007 S.W. Westwood Drive • Portland, Oregon 97239
(503) 293-8391 • (800) 240-8566 • www.sibylbooks.com

Originally published by Culinary Arts Ltd. 1987, revised 1994. Revised and expanded in 2002 by Sibyl Publications, Inc.

Graphic Design: *Design Studio Selby*

Printed in Canada

6 5 4 3 2 1

Cataloging in Publication

    Sawyer, Helene, 1946-
       Gourmet Mustards : the how-tos of making and cooking
with mustards / Helene Sawyer and Cheryl Long
       c. pm. --(Creative cooking series)
       Includes index.
       "Now revised and expanded."
       ISBN: 1-889531-04-9

       1. Cookery (Mustard) 2. Mustard (Condiment)
    I. Long, Cheryl, 1941- II. Title.

    TX819.M87S28 2002   641.6'384
                  QB102-200479

From the publisher:

    Gourmet Mustards was previously published by Culinary Arts Ltd. In 1998 Sibyl Publications purchased all rights to *Gourmet Mustards, Gourmet Vinegars* and *Classic Liqueurs*. This presented an exciting opportunity to create a series of cookbooks on specialty subjects, called **CREATIVE COOKING SERIES**. We will be expanding into new areas with the lastest how-tos on specific foods. If you have comments or suggestions for upcoming titles, contact Sibyl Publications at 1-800-240-8566 or by email at ms@sibylbooks.com.

Gourmet MUSTARDS

CONTENTS

"A grain of mustard-seed,"
the sage replied,
"Found where none old or young has ever died,
Will cure the pain you carry in your side."

JOHN WHITE CHADWICK, *BUDDHA'S LESSON*

INTRODUCTION

Helene Sawyer started it all with her love of mustards and a flair for creative cooking. Mustards became her profession with the opening of Chateau d'Helene, a company specializing in gourmet mustards and spices. With growth came a new company, Gazzelle's Fine Foods, which expanded to give the world a taste of fine mustards.

After many years Gazzelle's closed its doors but Helene's wonderful knowledge on the subject and her gourmet mustard secrets are in this cookbook. She first worked on the project with Cheryl Long, a home economist, cookbook author and editor, for her first mustard cookbook. The association was a happy one and today this new revised edition from Sibyl Publications reflects that collaboration. This cookbook has more recipes, information, tips and good things than ever before.

One of the most creative fields of cooking is creating your own condiments. *Gourmet Mustards* shows you how to make some of the very best mustards anywhere at a fraction of the gourmet shop price. Clear directions guide you through a wide variety of specialty mustards that will fill your pantry to capacity. Don't forget they make great gifts.

While commonly thought of as just a condiment for hot dogs and sandwiches, you will see mustard is so much more. The mustard seed is a spice, along with cinnamon, cloves and nutmeg. As a spice, a new door is opened to its cooking possibilities. The tiny mustard seed blooms fully in this book, in homemade gourmet mustards of many varieties, to sauces, spice blends, appetizers, entrées, soups and even dessert. Enjoy your culinary adventure into the exotic flavors of mustard.

About the authors

Like many successful food writers, Helene Sawyer and Cheryl Long have a passion for good food. Both love to create and explore new flavors in their kitchens and have a background in science, ideal for experimentation.

Helene Sawyer was for many years the owner of a gourmet mustard company. She created new flavors of mustards which customers enjoyed for years. All of her favorite recipes are in this book with the recipes proportioned for the at-home cook. Today she enjoys a career as a Nuclear Medicine Technologist but admits she still can't cook without her favorite condiment, mustard.

Cheryl Long is a Home Economist (George Fox University) and the author of several other cookbooks (*Classic Liqueurs, Easy Microwave Preserving*), and worked with Helene as editor in earlier editions of this mustard classic. In this expanded edition she joins Helene in creating new recipes for mustard lovers. Both authors live with their families in Oregon.

Acknowledgments

To Robert and Bruce Word for many years of taste testing. To Leslie, Viki, Dottie and Jan for their assistance. To Jill Stanford and Cheryl Long for their work on the earlier edition. To Miriam Selby who brought it all together for us in this wonderful new revised edition.

Basics of MUSTARD MAKING

The origin of the name "mustard" comes from the way it was originally made combined with ancient Latin and French words. The crushed seeds of various plants of the cabbage family were mixed with freshly pressed grape juice — the "must." The Latin word for "new wine" is mustum and the later French word — moustarde. From these old languages must-ard came into our vocabulary.

About Equipment

You will probably find all the equipment you need right in your own kitchen. One basic rule to note in mustard making is to avoid contact between mustard paste and aluminum. The presence of vinegar, wine or other acidic materials can leach metal molecules from aluminium pans. Use only plastic, glass, enameled or stainless steel utensils for making your mustards. For storage and aging of mustards, use only glass jars with tight-fitting plastic or enamel-lined lids.

Mustard Making Equipment

Plastic or stainless steel measuring spoons

Plastic or stainless steel mixing spoons

Plastic or stainless steel strainer or colander

Plastic, stainless steel or glass measuring cups, $1/4$- to 2-cup size

Plastic or rubber spatula

Blender or food processor

Cheesecloth for garni bags and straining

All equipment used should be completely free of grease or other contamination. Put utensils through a full dishwasher cycle or wash all items with hot, soapy water, then rinse in very hot, clear water.

Equipment for Storing

Glass jars in 4-, 6- or 8-ounce sizes

Plastic or enamel-lined metal lids

Labels

Fabric, yarn or ribbon to decorate your jars as gifts

Mustards

For superb gourmet mustards, start with good quality products. Knowing the different types of mustard seeds is key to producing the flavors you desire. The black seed is actually brown and, in fact, the white variety is really yellow in color.

White mustard seed (Brassica alba) is the most widely used seed. It is used in making pickles, relishes and recipes such as corned beef, where whole seed is required, as well as in making mustards. The white seed has almost no volatile oil; therefore, dry mustard is usually a combination of both black and white seeds.

Black seeds (Brassica nigra) are much smaller and more pungent than the white seed. True Dijon-style mustard uses a "black" mustard seed to achieve its spicy flavor.

Brown seed (Brassica juncea) is the hottest of the three types of mustard seeds. It is used in its ground form to make hot Chinese mustard and in hot curries.

Herbs, Spices, Vegetables, Fruits and Wines

All ingredients used should be of high quality. When fresh herbs are required, choose leaves with no wilted or browned edges. Fresh herbs should be washed and patted dry before chopping. When using dried herbs, take a look at the product and check to see that it appears fresh. Dried herbs that have been around too long lose their deep color and appear "washed out." Herbs need to be vital as they lose the oils in their leaves as they age, especially if they have not been properly sealed and stored. It's these precious oils that will be released in the mustard recipe, giving its special flavor!

When using spices, use the freshest possible. A jar of cinnamon that's been sitting on the shelf for three years has lost a lot of its punch. Replace your spices

frequently so they don't become old and flavorless.

The same rule applies to all fruit: choose the brightest, plumpest and juiciest. In citrus fruit the skin, or zest, is where the highly flavored oils are. Avoid fruits with any brown spots, and reap the full flavor.

Some recipes call for vegetables, such as onions or shallots. Again, they need to be bruise-free, plump and juicy, so that all their flavors will be released into the recipe.

If a recipe calls for wine, be sure it is of good quality. We use a dry white wine, a vermouth, in most recipes calling for "white wine." For red wines, we prefer a dry, full-bodied red. The Italian and Spanish reds are good, as is a French Bordeaux. For sherries and champagne, choose dry, rather than sweet ones.

Oils

Unless specified most recipes simply call for a vegetable oil so that you can choose the cooking oil you prefer. For most mustard recipes select an oil without a distinctive flavor of its own such as canola, safflower or soybean. For salad dressings you may prefer a flavorful olive oil, the choice is yours.

Whole or Powdered Mustard Seeds

In making your own gourmet mustards you may use whole mustard seeds and grind them to a powder yourself or purchase dry powdered mustard. There are two methods. Grind dry seeds in a blender, small food processor, electric coffee grinder (kept just for that purpose), spice grinder or use a mortar and pestle. Remember that by crushing the mustard seed, you have just released its volatile oils so handle carefully, avoid eye contact with oils. Dry whole mustard seeds produce about twice their volume when ground to a powder.

Whole mustard seeds may also be soaked for 24 to 48 hours to plump them. Cold water is the preferred liquid for soaking, however other liquids — all kinds

of vinegars, beers, sakes, wines or even liquor, such as rum or whiskey, may be used. In this method, combine the plumped seeds with needed liquid in a food processor or blender to the desired texture and proceed with your recipe.

Aging, Storing and Shelf Life

Newly prepared mustard is at its most pungent state, hot and bitey. It's quite like Chinese hot mustard that is made up just before it is served. At this point, if you prefer this degree of pungency, refrigerate your mustard after transferring it to a clean sterile jar. Refrigeration retards a decrease in pungency.

For a milder mustard, allow it to age, unrefrigerated. Our recommendation is to place the mustard in a jar and seal it with a tight-fitting enamel-lined lid. Store it in a cool, dark place, age it 3 to 8 weeks or longer if you still prefer a little less bite. At the point you find the pungency or degree of hotness that you like, refrigerate your jar of mustard.

Some of the mustard recipes in this book start with a prepared Dijon-style mustard base, with other flavors added. The base may be either the Basic Dijon-Style Mustard from our recipe or a ready-made Dijon from the store. Once you use either of these bases to create a new mustard flavor, it must be aged at room temperature for at least two weeks to allow the flavors to mingle. Taste after aging to evaluate the pungency. If you prefer a milder mustard, age another two weeks, then test again. Once the mustard reaches the level of mildness you enjoy, refrigerate.

The reason mustard is refrigerated now is to retard the loss of pungency and the process of oxidation. This process is what turns a yellow/gold mustard into a dark brown, non eye-appealing condiment. The only time it is quite necessary to refrigerate mustard is when the recipe calls for eggs or fresh vegetables such as onion, shallots, etc.

With the exception of the refrigerated mustards just mentioned, it is true that no matter what its age, mustard does not seem to grow mold, mildew or harmful bacteria. It may dry out, lose its flavor and turn dark brown from oxidation, but even so, can be considered edible, if unappetizing. If it dries out, the addition of wine or vinegar will reconstitute it.

The shelf life of mustard is indefinite. This is one food that is extremely versatile. You can make it up a couple of months before giving it as a gift, or whip up a batch at the last minute, providing you give aging instructions to the recipient. Be sure and give refrigeration instructions as well to the recipient if needed.

Mustard: A Low-Cal Spice

Mustard is a wonderful spice and flavoring for so many foods as you will see in this cookbook. It also has the special quality of having almost no calories. This attribute makes mustard the dieter's friend. Even if you are not dieting you are probably often looking for foods that are lower in fat, cholesterol and sodium. Most of the mustard recipes fill this bill nicely. A few recipes call for small amounts of oil or salt. Hot Swedish-Style Mustard calls for eggs, however we have included a low-cholesterol Swedish mustard variation if you prefer. We have recipes for the calorie conscious and those preferring low fat, cholesterol or sodium as well as richer recipes for special occasions. Low-calorie recipes in this book include content information on calorie count, fat, cholesterol and sodium and are marked with a Lo-Cal symbol.

Cooking with mustard opens up a world of new flavors you may not have explored before. So relax, enjoy and spread the mustard on thickly!

Food Substitutes

Often substitutions are needed in cooking, especially if you desire to lower the calories, fat, cholesterol or sodium. We show many of these. Here are some suggestions for our favorite substitutions.

FOOD	SUBSTITUTE
butter	*margarine (for cooking use regular margarine)*
cheese	*low-fat or tofu non-dairy varieties*
cream	*skim evaporated milk, undiluted*
whipped cream	*whipped cream substitute or non-fat sour cream*
egg	*egg white or egg substitute*
egg yolk	*1 whole egg or egg substitute*
mayonnaise	*light, low-fat or eggless mayonnaise*
milk	*non-dairy soy milk or chicken broth (for potato dishes)*
whole milk	*evaporated milk, diluted with equal amount of water or 2% milk*
oil (for baking)	*applesauce or prune purée*
oil (for coating)	*vegetable oil spray*
pie crust (for quiche)	*cooked potato slices (red preferred) with peel*
salt	*lemon juice (for most foods)*
sour cream	*light or non-fat sour cream, low- or non-fat yogurt*
sugar	*honey (1 cup sugar = $^7/_8$ cup honey) or sugar substitute*
wheat flour	*spelt flour*

"A tale without love is like beef without mustard: an insipid dish."
ANATOLE FRANCE, French humorist

*In the United States, the present consumption of mustard
is greater than every other spice except pepper.*

MAKING Gourmet MUSTARDS

With the directions and recipes in this book you will be able to fill your pantry with a selection of gourmet mustards. Soon you will be replacing regular prepared mustards with some of your favorite homemade gourmet mustards. You will also be able to create some of your own original gourmet mustards. We hope you receive as much enjoyment from this creative process as we have!

When making mustards, remember that using vinegar instead of water in a mustard recipe weakens the enzyme reaction and produces a milder, less biting mustard. Water may be called for when a very hot mustard is desired, such as in Chinese Hot Mustard. Thus, you can control the hotness by the ingredients used as well as in the aging. Salt, vinegar and wine actually help preserve the strength of the mustard so that it retains its flavor for a very long time.

Adding a touch of gourmet mustard gives foods that subtle extra taste good cooks strive for. Your friends will probably ask for your secrets.

We may shatter a lot of beliefs when we say that the inexpensive, bright yellow "hot-dog style" mustard should not be considered the "basic" mustard for cooking purposes. Oh, it tastes great — on hot dogs! In fact, nothing else would be quite right. But for cooking, the Dijon-style mustard is far superior, because of its ability to enhance so many flavors.

The gourmet mustards and the special food recipes in this book are very giftable. Give a special mustard as a gift with a recipe tag tied to the container. Enjoy!

Basic Dijon-Style Mustard

A culinary classic!   YIELD: 1½ CUPS

>   2 cups dry white wine
>   1 large onion, chopped
>   3 cloves garlic, crushed
>   1 cup dry mustard
>   3 tablespoons honey
>   1 tablespoon vegetable oil
>   2 teaspoons salt

Combine wine, onion and garlic in a saucepan. Heat to boiling and simmer
5 minutes. Cool and discard strained solids. Add this liquid to dry mustard,
stirring constantly until smooth. Blend in honey, oil and salt. Return to saucepan
(have hankies ready or hold face away from steam), heat slowly until thickened,
stirring constantly. Cool, store in a jar with a tight-fitting lid. Place in refrigerator.

Now the fun and creativity begin!

Let your cooking skills take you into a new world by just adding a few simple
ingredients to your finished Dijon-style mustard. Or for an easy head start, buy
a jar of good Dijon mustard and start your creativity there. See how simple, yet
elegant, the following recipes can be.

Aioli-Garlic Mustard

Here's a great one for garlic lovers! YIELD: 1 CUP

> 1 cup Dijon-style mustard
> 3 large cloves garlic, minced
> 1 teaspoon vegetable oil

Combine all ingredients. Transfer to a jar with a tight-fitting lid. Refrigerate.

Honey Dijon Mustard

A favorite: hot and tangy-sweet. YIELD: ABOUT 2 CUPS

> 1 cup honey
> 1 cup Dijon-style mustard
> ¾ cup dry mustard

Combine ingredients. Transfer to a jar with a tight-fitting lid. Refrigerate.

VARIATIONS

Mild Honey Mustard

Decrease honey to ¼ cup and omit dry mustard. Proceed as directed above.

Sweet Tarragon Mustard

Decrease honey to ¼ cup and omit dry mustard. Add ¼ cup fresh finely minced tarragon leaves or 2 tablespoons dried, crushed. Proceed as directed above.

White Wine Mustard

A sophisticated, spicy mustard. If you like it sweeter, double the sugar. YIELD: ABOUT 1 CUP

> 1/3 cup white wine, dry preferred
> 1/4 cup white wine vinegar
> 1/4 cup dry mustard
> 1 tablespoon powdered sugar
> 1/2 teaspoon salt
> 1 egg or equivalent egg substitute

Combine wine, wine vinegar, mustard, sugar and salt in a small bowl. When well mixed, cover and let sit for several hours or overnight.

Place mixture in top of a double boiler, over pot of simmering water. Whisk in egg; continue until mustard becomes thickened, about 3 to 5 minutes. Remove from heat, let cool to room temperature. Serve or refrigerate.

Christmas Mustard

An unusual, spicy and giftable mustard.   YIELD: 1 CUP

> 1 cup Dijon-style mustard
> 1 tablespoon minced crystallized ginger
> 1 tablespoon minced mixed candied fruit
> 1/8 teaspoon ground cinnamon
> 1/4 teaspoon ground cloves

Mix all ingredients, transfer to jar with a tight-fitting lid. Age in a cool dark place 2 weeks. Store in refrigerator.

Cranberry Mustard

Love that sweet tart flavor? Here is a sweet, tart and somewhat hot mustard. Perfect at Thanksgiving, but enjoy it year round.   YIELD: ABOUT 2 CUPS

> 1 cup Dijon-style mustard
> 3/4 cup jellied cranberry sauce
> 3/4 cup dry mustard

Combine all the ingredients, whisk until smooth. Transfer to a jar with a tight-fitting lid. Refrigerate.

Fenberry or Cranberry II Mustard

In the early days in Britain, Fenberry was the name used for Cranberry. The berry comes from the Honeysuckle family. Wonderful on poultry sandwiches.   YIELD: ABOUT 2 CUPS

> 1 cup Dijon-style mustard
> 1 tablespoon honey
> 2 tablespoons cranberry liqueur*
>   (optional, but if you've got it, do try it!)
> 3/4 cup whole cranberry sauce
> 3/4 cup dry mustard
> 1 large shallot, chopped

Combine all ingredients except shallot; mix until smooth. Stir in shallot. Transfer to a jar with a tight-fitting lid and refrigerate.

* The recipe for a beautiful **Cranberry Liqueur** is in the book, *Classic Liqueurs*, by Cheryl Long and Heather Kibbey, if you want to make your own.

Lemon, Lime or Orange Mustard

Choose your favorite citrus flavor or combination for this fresh, zesty mustard that's great in sauces.   YIELD: ABOUT 1 CUP

> 1 cup Dijon-style mustard
> 1 tablespoon fresh lemon, lime or orange juice
> 2 teaspoons honey
> grated peel (zest) of a lemon, lime or orange

Mix all ingredients in a medium bowl. Transfer to a jar with a tight-fitting lid. Store in a cool dark place for 2 weeks, then refrigerate.

Hawaiian Mustard

A remembrance of paradise.   YIELD: ABOUT 1 1/2 CUPS

> 1 cup Dijon-style mustard
> 1/4 cup drained crushed pineapple
> 1/4 cup flaked coconut
> 1 tablespoon soy sauce

Mix ingredients in a small bowl. Transfer to a jar with a tight-fitting lid. Age in a cool dark place for 2 weeks, then refrigerate.

Gourmet Onion Mustard

Try Vidalia, Texas Sweet, Burmuda, Walla Walla, Maui or a favorite garden onion for a distinctive taste! Excellent with meats, poultry and cheeses.   YIELD: ABOUT 2 CUPS

I cup Dijon-style mustard
½ cup dry mustard
½ cup white wine vinegar
½ cup chopped onion

Combine all ingredients, transfer to jar with a tight-fitting lid. Age in a cool dark place for 2 weeks. Store in refrigerator.

Shallot Mustard

Lightly flavored with shallots. Very good with beef.   YIELD: ABOUT I CUP

I cup Dijon-style mustard
3 large shallots, finely chopped

Mix ingredients. Transfer to jar with a tight-fitting lid. Age in a cool dark place for 2 to 8 weeks, then refrigerate.

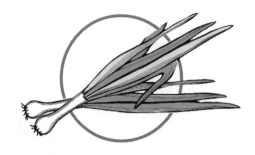

Italian Supremo Mustard

A fantastic topping for juicy grilled Italian sausage on a bun. Add sautéed red peppers and onions, deliziosa!   YIELD: ABOUT 1 1/2 CUPS

I cup Dijon-style mustard
1/2 cup dry mustard
1/2 cup red wine
1/4 cup chopped sun-dried tomatoes
2 tablespoons chopped black olives
1/2 teaspoon garlic powder
1/4 teaspoon dried basil
1/4 teaspoon dried chervil
1/8 teaspoon dried cilantro

Mix all ingredients together. Transfer to jar with a tight-fitting lid. Refrigerate.

Barbecue Mustard

Use as you would barbecue sauce.   YIELD: ABOUT 2 CUPS

I cup Dijon-style mustard
1/2 cup of your favorite barbecue sauce
1/2 cup chopped onion
1/4 cup dry mustard
I clove garlic, minced
1/4 teaspoon liquid smoke

Combine all ingredients. Transfer to a jar with a tight-fitting lid and refrigerate.

Ginger Curry Mustard

This will give taste-buds a wake-up call.   YIELD: I CUP

2 tablespoons grated fresh ginger

I cup Dijon-style mustard

I tablespoon curry powder

I tablespoon rice wine vinegar

Peel ginger before grating. Combine all ingredients. Transfer to jar with a tight-fitting lid. Age in a cool dark place for 2 weeks. Store in refrigerator.

Tex-Mex Mustard

Spread this on top of chicken and bake for an easy and zesty dinner.

YIELD: ABOUT I ⅓ CUPS

I cup Dijon-style mustard

I (4-ounce) can chopped mild green chilies

¼ teaspoon garlic powder

¼ teaspoon onion powder

I tablespoon Tequila or dry white wine

2 tablespoon dry mustard

I teaspoon chopped fresh cilantro leaves

⅛ teaspoon cumin

⅛ teaspoon fresh ground coriander seeds

Mix all ingredients. Transfer to jar with a tight-fitting lid. Age 2 weeks in a cool, dark place. Store in refrigerator.

Hot Tex-Mex Mustard

Made with the hottest fresh pepper known. Caution: use gloves when preparing this fresh pepper.   YIELD: 1 1/4 CUPS

> 1 cup Dijon-style mustard
> 1 fresh Habañero pepper

Remove and discard half the seeds from pepper. Chop remaining seeds and pepper. Combine with mustard. Transfer to a jar, seal and refrigerate.

Cajun-Style Mustard

Hot and spicy Cajun-style.   YIELD: ABOUT 1 3/4 CUPS

> 1/4 cup whole brown mustard seeds
> 1/2 cup white or cider vinegar
> 1 cup Dijon-style mustard
> 1/4 cup dry mustard
> 3/4 teaspoon garlic powder
> 1/2 teaspoon onion powder
> 1/4 teaspoon dried ground basil
> 1/4 teaspoon ground black pepper
> 1/4 teaspoon ground cayenne pepper
> 1/4 teaspoon white pepper
> 1/4 teaspoon paprika

Soak brown mustard seeds in vinegar for 30 minutes. Combine all ingredients, transfer to jar with a tight-fitting lid. Age in a cool dark place for 2 weeks. Store in refrigerator.

Jalapeño Mustard

Hot! Adds great flavor to sauces too.   YIELD: ABOUT 1 CUP

2 canned jalapeño peppers, chopped (reserve liquid)
1 tablespoon reserved jalapeño liquid
1 cup Dijon-style mustard

Mix peppers and 1 tablespoon liquid with mustard. Transfer to a jar with a tight-fitting lid, seal. Age 2 to 8 weeks, then refrigerate.

Sesame Mustard

Sesame seeds add a nutty flavor. Asian-style sesame oil can be found in Oriental food sections or markets.   YIELD: ABOUT 1 1/2 CUPS

1 tablespoon grated ginger
1 cup Dijon-style mustard
1/4 cup dry mustard
1/4 cup sesame seeds
1 tablespoon soy sauce
1 clove garlic, finely minced
1 teaspoon sesame oil (Asian style)

Peel ginger before grating. Combine all ingredients. Transfer to a jar with a tight-fitting lid. Age in a cool, dark place for 2 weeks. Store in refrigerator.

Herbed Mustard

Vary the herbs to create your own special flavor. Use a single herb or a combination.

YIELD: 1 CUP

- 1 tablespoon of one of the following dried herbs:
  Herbes de Provence, tarragon, dill weed, lemon thyme, rosemary or basil
- 1 tablespoon dry vermouth
- 1 cup Dijon-style mustard

Combine herb of choice and vermouth in a medium bowl, let stand for 20 minutes. Gradually mix in mustard. Transfer to a jar with a tight-fitting lid. Store in a cool, dark place for 2 weeks, then refrigerate.

Energy, like the biblical grain of the mustard-seed, will remove mountains.

Three Herbs Mustard

This is a delicately flavored blend.

YIELD: ABOUT I CUP

¼ cup fresh parsley or 2 tablespoons dried
¼ cup fresh tarragon leaves or 2 tablespoons dried
¼ cup fresh dill weed or 2 tablespoons dried
I cup Dijon-style mustard
I tablespoon dry vermouth

When using fresh herbs, place in a food processor or blender and finely chop. Add mustard and vermouth, blend until smooth and creamy. When using dried herbs, mix herbs in a medium bowl and stir in mustard until well-blended. Transfer to a jar with a tight-fitting lid. Store in a cool, dark place for 2 weeks, then refrigerate.

Black Peppercorn Mustard

This mustard is to die for. Try it!

YIELD: ABOUT I ¼ CUPS

I cup Dijon-style mustard
I tablespoon rice wine vinegar
I tablespoon honey
2 tablespoons cracked black peppercorns
2 tablespoons dry mustard

Combine all ingredients. Transfer to a jar with a tight-fitting lid. Let flavors blend in refrigerator at least a day before serving.

Green Peppercorn Mustard

Delicious on pork chops, poached seafood or to spice up mayonnaise.

YIELD: ABOUT 2 CUPS

1/2 cup hot water

1/4 cup whole yellow mustard seed

I cup dry mustard

1/2 cup dry vermouth

1/4 cup honey

I teaspoon dried crumbled tarragon leaves

I teaspoon salt

1/8 teaspoon ground cloves

1/8 teaspoon ground allspice

1/8 cup green peppercorns

Combine water and mustard seed in a small bowl and let stand for one hour. Drain well. Transfer mustard seeds to a food processor or blender. Add remaining ingredients except peppercorns and purée, stop machine several times to scrape down sides of the container (mixture will be coarse). Add peppercorns and blend. Transfer to a jar with a tight-fitting lid. Age in a cool dark place for 2 to 8 weeks, then refrigerate.

Apricot Mustard

This is exotic. Great with stout cheese.   YIELD: 2 CUPS

I cup Sweet 'N' Hot Mustard
1/2 cup apricot jam
3/4 cup dry mustard
3 dried apricots, minced

Combine all ingredients. Transfer to a jar with a tight-fitting lid and refrigerate.

Berry Mustard

Fruit mustards have their own special charm.   YIELD: ABOUT 2 CUPS

I cup Sweet 'N' Hot Mustard
1/2 cup seeded, puréed berries (such as raspberries,
   marionberries, boysenberries, etc.)
1/4 cup honey
I cup dry mustard

Combine all ingredients. Transfer to a jar with a tight-fitting lid. Refrigerate.

Champagne Mustard

A very giftable mustard. We recommend aging this one 3 to 4 months for a more delicate flavor. YIELD: ABOUT 1 1/2 CUPS

> 1 cup dry mustard
> 1/2 cup powdered sugar
> 1/2 teaspoon salt
> 3/4 cup (6 ounces) flat champagne
> 1 tablespoon fresh lemon juice

Place all ingredients in a food processor or blender and mix until smooth. Stop frequently to scrape down sides. Transfer to a jar with a tight-fitting lid. Age in a cool dark place 3 to 4 months, then refrigerate.

VARIATIONS

Champagne Dill Mustard

Add 2 tablespoons dill weed to the basic recipe.

Champagne Honey Mustard

Substitute 1/4 cup honey for the powdered sugar in the basic recipe.

Champagne Shallot Mustard

Add 3 tablespoons chopped shallots to the basic recipe; refrigerate.

Red Wine Mustard

A hearty, herb-flavored Italian-style mustard.   YIELD: ABOUT 2 CUPS

I cup dry mustard

½ cup packed brown sugar

½ cup red wine, dry Italian or Cabernet preferred

I tablespoon of one of the following dried herbs:
  rosemary, oregano, marjoram, basil or a combination

½ teaspoon salt

⅓ cup vegetable oil

Put all ingredients, except oil, in a food processor or blender; combine until creamy. With the machine running, add oil through the feed tube in a slow, steady stream. Blend until consistency of mayonnaise. Stop machine occasionally to scrape down sides of the work bowl. Pour into a jar with a tight-fitting lid. Age in a cool dark place for 2 to 8 weeks, refrigerate.

English Pub Mustard

In Britain this is made up fresh each day to serve with bangers, cold cuts, meat pies and chops. Dry mustard when first mixed with liquid releases its oil and is at its hottest! From that point it starts to cool down. YIELD: ABOUT 1 ½ CUPS

1 cup dry mustard

½ cup packed brown sugar

1 teaspoon salt

¼ teaspoon turmeric

¾ cup (6 ounces) flat beer or ale

Put mustard, sugar, salt and turmeric in a food processor or blender and mix well. With the machine running, add the beer through the feed tube slowly but in a steady stream. Blend until smooth and creamy, stopping the machine frequently to scrape down the sides of the work bowl. Transfer to a jar with a tight-fitting lid. Age in a cool dark place for 2 weeks. Store in refrigerator.

"What say you to a piece of beef and mustard?"
SHAKESPEARE

Bavarian Brown Mustard

This is a grainy, Bavarian-style mustard. Excellent on all types of wieners and sausages.

YIELD: ABOUT 1 1/2 CUPS

1/2 cup whole brown mustard seed

3/4 cup dry sherry

1 cup dry mustard

1/4 cup packed brown sugar

1/4 teaspoon salt

Combine mustard seed and sherry in a medium bowl and let stand for 2 to 3 hours. Transfer mixture to a food processor or blender and blend until almost smooth (mustard will be grainy). Add the dry mustard, sugar and salt; blend well. Place in a jar with a tight-fitting lid. Age in a cool dark place 2 to 8 weeks. Store in a cool dark place.

Chinese Hot Mustard

Serve with egg rolls, won ton and fried shrimp. For the hottest Chinese Hot Mustard eliminate the aging period and serve immediately. Commercial dry powdered mustard may be used or you may grind any combination of mustard seeds to produce the degree of hotness you desire.

YIELD: ABOUT 1 CUP

1 cup dry mustard

3/4 cup water

Mix ingredients in a small bowl. Small amounts of additional water may be added for the consistency you desire. Transfer to a jar with a tight-fitting lid. Age in a cool dark place for 2 weeks, then refrigerate.

Hot Swedish-Style Mustard

Wonderful on all types of cold cuts, wieners and sausages. This mustard thickens as it sits overnight.   YIELD: ABOUT 1½ CUPS

> 3 eggs
> ¼ cup packed brown sugar
> ½ cup honey
> ⅓ cup apple cider or juice
> ⅓ cup apple cider vinegar
> 1 cup dry mustard
> ½ teaspoon salt
> ¼ teaspoon ground cardamom
> ¼ teaspoon ground cloves
> ¼ teaspoon ground cinnamon
> ¼ teaspoon ground mace, optional

Beat eggs in a large, non-aluminium saucepan. Add remaining ingredients and mix well. Cook over low heat, stirring until mixture thickens, about 10 minutes. Cool, then refrigerate.

VARIATION

Low-Cholesterol Swedish Mustard

For those watching cholesterol, leave out the egg yolks and just use the whites. You may have to add a little more dry mustard if you think the mixture is not thickening. The only difference we have found is in the color of the finished mustard. This variation has a pale amber color, while the original recipe is a richer, deeper amber color. There is no taste difference.

Sweet 'N' Hot Mustard

Great with pâtés, ham, meat loaf or pork. Or, try some mixed with peanut butter for a real flavor pick-up!   YIELD: ABOUT 2 CUPS

3 tablespoons anise or fennel seed

1 ½ cups dry mustard

¾ cup packed brown sugar

¾ cup apple cider vinegar

1 ½ teaspoons salt

½ cup vegetable oil

Process anise or fennel seed in a food processor or blender until crushed, about 3 minutes. Add mustard, sugar, vinegar and salt; mix well. Stop frequently to scrape down sides of the work bowl. With the machine running, add oil in a slow, steady stream and blend until the mixture is the consistency of mayonnaise. Transfer to a jar with a tight-fitting lid. Age in a cool dark place for 2 to 8 weeks, then refrigerate.

"Johnson's conversation was by much too strong for
a person accustomed to obsequiousness and flattery;
it was mustard in a young child's mouth."

BOSWELL ON JOHNSON

Horseradish-Lovers Mustard

Requests for a horseradish mustard recipe outnumber all others two to one!

YIELD: ABOUT 1½ CUPS

1 cup dry mustard
½ cup powdered sugar
½ teaspoon salt
½ cup white wine vinegar
¼ cup vegetable oil
1 tablespoon fresh lemon juice
¼ teaspoon grated lemon peel (zest)
5 tablespoons prepared horseradish

Put all ingredients in a food processor or blender and mix well. Scrape down the sides of the work bowl frequently. Transfer to a jar with a tight-fitting lid. Age in a cool dark place 2 to 8 weeks, then refrigerate.

Coney Island Style Mustard

"Take me out to the ball game ... " This is the classic ballpark mustard.

YIELD: ABOUT 1 1/4 CUPS

3/4 cup basic prepared bright yellow mustard
1/4 cup ketchup
1/2 cup chopped onion
1 tablespoon sweet pickle relish

Mix all ingredients, transfer to a jar with a tight-fitting lid. Age in a cool dark place for 2 weeks. Store in refrigerator.

Smokey Mustard

The flavor of an open campfire comes through on this one.   YIELD: ABOUT 1 1/4 CUPS

1 cup basic prepared bright yellow mustard
1/4 cup dry mustard
1 tablespoon liquid smoke or to taste
1/2 teaspoon onion powder

Mix all ingredients, transfer to a jar with a tight-fitting lid. Age in a cool dark place for 2 weeks. Store in refrigerator.

Mustard Plaster

Old-fashioned mustard plasters have been around for generations. It is said to help break up congestion due to a cold. While we make no claims for curing colds, here is an authentic recipe.

I tablespoon dry mustard
4 tablespoons flour
water as needed

Mix mustard and flour with enough water to make a smooth paste. Spread the paste on a clean white cotton cloth and fold the cloth in half with the mustard mixture inside. Place on chest just below neck. Leave on chest until skin turns pink — about 5 to 10 minutes. Be careful not to burn the skin by leaving it on too long. Remove, wipe chest dry and rub down with rubbing alcohol to close pores. Repeat on back over the shoulder blades.

Mustard Fomentation

An old remedy said to be good for aches and pains. Prepare the mustard liquid as directed then dip a towel into the hot liquid, wring it out and apply it on the painful area for several minutes. Next, apply a cold water compress, then repeat with a hot mustard towel.

4 cups boiling water
1/3 cup crushed mustard seeds

In a large covered pot, bring water to a boil. When boiling, stir in seeds. Re-cover pot, remove from heat. Let brew 10 minutes. Strain liquid into bowl, discarding seeds. When correct temperature, place a small towel into liquid, wring out and apply as needed.

TIP: To reheat a wet towel, place in microwave for I minute on High.

*"The new Condiment King of Camp Dudley is Adam Chamberlain.
Adam ate a bowl of relish, a bowl of ketchup and a bowl of mustard."*

ANONYMOUS YMCA CAMP COUNSELOR

COOKING
WITH
Gourmet
MUSTARDS

MUSTARD BUTTERS and OILS

RUBS and SPICE BLENDS

SAUCES and TOPPINGS

It is not necessary to be an experienced cook to use gourmet mustards. Just remember that mustard is a spice as well as a condiment. Using that premise, begin to add mustard to some of your favorite recipes. Try the recipes in this book as your guide. Above all, don't be afraid to experiment!

MUSTARD BUTTER

This is one of the chef's best secrets for adding a special flavor to hot grilled meats, seafood or cooked vegetables. Place a slice onto piping hot food before serving. Also adds zing when used as a spread on appetizers, hot breads or sandwiches.

YIELD: ABOUT ½ CUP

1 ½ tablespoons dry powdered mustard

lemon juice

dash white pepper

½ cup (1 stick) butter, salted or unsalted, softened

Combine dry mustard with a little lemon juice to make a soft paste. Whisk mustard paste and pepper into softened butter. Place mixture on waxed paper, forming a roll. Chill. Slice or spread for use. Store in refrigerator.

VARIATION

Dill Mustard Butter

Prepare Mustard Butter as directed. Add dill by sprinkling chopped fresh or dried dill over sliced butter before serving. Or coat butter roll with dill, then slice. Top hot seafood with a slice of Dill Mustard Butter before serving.

HERBED MUSTARD BUTTER

A wonderful herbal variation that changes flavors with the type of mustard and herbs you choose.   YIELD: ABOUT ½ CUP

>   1 to 6 teaspoons any gourmet mustard
>   dash Worcestershire sauce
>   lemon juice
>   ½ cup (1 stick) butter, salted or unsalted, softened
>   chopped fresh parsley, dill weed or chives

Combine mustard, Worcestershire and and enough lemon juice to make a paste. Add butter, mixing well. Shape into a log or ball. Refrigerate a bit if too soft. Roll log in chopped herb. Wrap in plastic wrap and refrigerate until needed. Slice or spread for use. Store in refrigerator.

HERB AND MUSTARD SEED OIL

A richly flavored oil that brings the distinctive taste of mustard when added to beef, pork or poultry as well as to special salad dressings. A mortar and pestle work well for crushing the mustard seeds or use a small bowl and the back of a wooden spoon. Herbs add their own distinctive flavor. Some to try are fresh basil, dill, oregano, rosemary or tarragon.   YIELD: 1 CUP

>   2 tablespoons whole mustard seeds, any variety
>   ¼ cup fresh herbs of choice
>   1 cup olive or vegetable oil

Crush mustard seeds slightly and set aside. Rinse and pat fresh herbs to dry. Chop herb coarsely and combine with oil in a small saucepan. Heat mixture over medium-high heat, stirring frequently until hot. Let cool. Add crushed mustard seeds to oil mixture, stirring well. Let mixture sit for 30 minutes for flavors to blend; strain. Pour strained oil into a sterilized glass jar and cover tightly. Use immediately or store in the refrigerator. Use oil within 1 week.

CREAMY MUSTARD SAUCE

Serve with cooked vegetables, such as broccoli, cabbage or carrots, or with ham or fish.   YIELD: 1 CUP

1 cup regular or light sour cream
1 tablespoon prepared herb or Dijon-style mustard
1 tablespoon finely minced onion
1/4 teaspoon salt
1/8 teaspoon white pepper

In small saucepan over low heat, combine sour cream, mustard, onion, salt and pepper. Heat through. Serve over hot, drained vegetables.

CURRANT SAUCE

Easy to make, versatile and delicious! This sauce is used for the Shrimp and Snow Peas appetizer, however you can use it for a variety of foods. Try as a glaze for meatballs or chicken or dip chicken wings in it. An interesting substitute for Sweet and Sour Sauce to go with many Oriental foods.   YIELD: 3/4 CUP

1/4 cup Dijon-style mustard
1/2 cup red currant jelly

Mix together, wait 5 minutes and mix or whisk again. Can be served warm or at room temperature.

If you want the pungency of mustard, add it at the end of the cooking period and keep the heat low. Do not boil.

MUSTARD DILL SAUCE

Serve this hot or cold with seafood or vegetables.   YIELD: ABOUT 1 CUP

1 cup milk
1 egg yolk or equivalent egg substitute
1 tablespoon dry powdered mustard
1 tablespoon white vinegar
1 teaspoon sugar
1/2 teaspoon dried dill weed
1/4 teaspoon salt
dash white pepper

Whisk milk and egg yolk together. Whisk in all remaining ingredients. Cook in double boiler or over a very low heat, stirring constantly until thickened.

MUSTARD WINE MARINADE

An excellent marinade for beef, pork or lamb.   YIELD: ABOUT 1 CUP

1/2 cup dry red wine
2 tablespoons lemon juice
1/4 cup Dijon-Style, Gourmet Onion or mustard of choice
1 tablespoon freshed chopped rosemary or 1/2 teaspoon dried
1 clove garlic, crushed
1/2 teaspoon coarsely ground black pepper
1 tablespoon olive oil

Combine all ingredients. Pour over meat, cover and refrigerate for 2 to 24 hours before cooking.

ZINGY MUSTARD SAUCE

A taste tingler that sparkles with roast beef. YIELD: ABOUT $3/4$ CUP

- 2 egg yolks
- 2 tablespoons Herbes de Provence, Bavarian Brown or Green Peppercorn mustard
- 2 tablespoons white wine vinegar
- 1 tablespoon prepared horseradish
- 1 tablespoon sugar
- 1 tablespoon white wine
- 1 tablespoon butter or margarine
- $1/2$ teaspoon salt
- $1/2$ cup whipping cream

Combine all ingredients, except cream, in a small saucepan; mix well. Cook over low heat until sauce thickens, about 2 minutes. Remove from heat, stir until smooth and cool. Whip cream and fold into cooled mixture. Serve. Refrigerate any leftover sauce.

QUICK SEAFOOD COCKTAIL SAUCE

Make your own zesty cocktail sauce economically. YIELD: ABOUT 1/2 CUP

> 1/2 cup ketchup
> juice of one medium lemon
> 1/2 teaspoon Dijon-style mustard
> 1/4 teaspoon creamed horseradish
> dash salt, optional

Blend all ingredients together. Chill. Store in refrigerator.

DILL MUSTARD SEAFOOD SAUCE

Spoon this sauce on any white fish. YIELD: 1 CUP, ENOUGH SAUCE FOR TWO POUNDS OF FISH

> 1 cup sour cream, regular or light
> 1 to 2 teaspoons dry powdered mustard, to taste
> 1/2 teaspoon dried dill weed
> 1/4 teaspoon lemon pepper
> 1/4 teaspoon salt

Combine all ingredients until well blended. Set aside. Broil or bake fish. Spread sauce over cooked fish. Place under broiler for a few minutes for sauce to heat and brown slightly. Serve.

CREOLE REMOULADE SAUCE

This sauce brings back memories of New Orleans and the wonderful shrimp there. A perfect sauce for crab or shrimp cocktails.   YIELD: ABOUT 3 1/2 CUPS

1 1/2 teaspoons hot sauce

1 tablespoon prepared horseradish

1 tablespoon Worcestershire sauce

3 tablespoon capers, drained

1/4 cup ketchup

1/4 cup lemon juice

1/4 cup chopped green onions

1/2 cup Green Peppercorn, Bavarian Brown, Hot Swedish-Style, Horseradish Lovers or any Dijon-based mustard

1/2 cup chopped fresh parsley

3/4 cup minced celery

2 cups regular or light mayonnaise

Combine all ingredients and refrigerate until well chilled. Serve cold. Refrigerate any leftover sauce.

FRENCH MUSTARD SAUCE

This special sauce is quite hot, similar to Chinese Hot Mustard. It is delicious with roast beef, pork, hot dogs or sausages.   YIELD: 1/2 CUP

> 1/2 cup dry mustard
> 1/4 cup beer
> I tablespoon red wine vinegar
> 1/2 teaspoon salt

Combine all ingredients in a bowl. Serve.

LIME SAUCE

This is our favorite sauce for baked or poached fish. Wonderful on baked halibut, grilled salmon or stuffed sole.   YIELD: ABOUT I CUP

> 2 tablespoons butter
> 2 shallots, minced
> 3/4 cup white wine, Chardonnay preferred
> I cup heavy cream
> I tablespoon Lime Mustard

Over medium heat, melt butter in sauté pan. Sauté shallots until transparent. Add wine and cook until volume is reduced by half. Turn heat to low, add cream slowly, stirring constantly until reduced to desired consistency. Add mustard. Serve immediately. Refrigerate any leftovers.

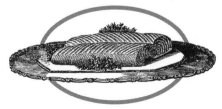

SUPERB MUSTARD COATING FOR HAM

A different topping for ham that has always been a hit. Add coating to ham during the last 20 minutes of baking time. YIELD: ABOUT 1/3 CUP

2 tablespoons dry mustard

1/2 tablespoon cornstarch

1 egg yolk

1 tablespoon Lime, Apricot, Sweet 'N' Hot, Cranberry
or Honey mustard

fine fresh bread crumbs

Mix all ingredients except bread crumbs. Spread mustard coating over top and sides of ham. Sprinkle bread crumbs over. Return ham to oven for 20 minutes.

HORSERADISH MUSTARD SAUCE

Superb with corned beef. YIELD: ABOUT 3/4 CUP

2 tablespoons prepared horseradish

2 tablespoons white wine vinegar

2 tablespoons Lime, Tarragon or Horseradish Lovers mustard

dash of cayenne

1/2 cup whipping cream

Combine all ingredients except whipping cream in a small bowl. Whip cream to soft peaks, fold into mustard mixture. Serve. Refrigerate any leftover sauce.

> *"Condiments are like old friends –*
> *highly thought of, but often taken for granted."*
> MARILYN KAYTOR

SPICY MUSTARD TOPPING

This is a wonderful topping for vegetables or fish. Omit cheese for fish. This is used for the Spicy Crowned Vegetable Platter recipe that is a dinner party spectacular. People who don't like vegetables eat them with this topping! YIELD: ½ CUP

½ cup mayonnaise, regular, light or non-fat

1 teaspoon dry powdered mustard

1 tablespoon fresh minced onion or 1 ½ teaspoons dry

½ cup shredded cheese, Cheddar or Jalapeño Jack

Prepare topping by combining mayonnaise, mustard and onion. Set aside to allow flavors to blend for at least 15 minutes. Reserve cheese.

Top cooked vegetables or fish with topping. Sprinkle cheese over vegetables, (omit for fish) and heat under broiler or in microwave for 1 minute, just until cheese melts a little. Serve.

A survey in France in 1812 revealed that 93 different kinds of mustards were available!

HERB-MUSTARD RUB

Use on poultry or meats. Mix fresh or dried herbs with your favorite mustards for a richly flavorful coating for roasted poultry or meats. Vary ingredients for different flavors. Try mild sweet onions or red onions for color. Herbs such as fresh basil, lemon thyme or oregano add their own unique flavors. Combine herbs as you prefer.

YIELD: ½ CUP (ENOUGH FOR 4 TO 6 SERVINGS)

I small onion, finely minced

3 tablespoons Dijon-style, Honey Dijon or other mustard of choice

2 teaspoons fresh herbs of choice, chopped or ½ teaspoon dried

dash of ground black pepper

Combine all ingredients. Spread on poultry, beef, pork or lamb before roasting.

PICKLING SPICE MIX

Make your own pickling spice for pickling a variety of vegetables. YIELD: ABOUT ½ CUP

2 tablespoons allspice

2 tablespoons whole coriander

2 tablespoons whole white or yellow mustard seeds

I tablespoon crushed bay leaves

I tablespoon crushed cinnamon sticks

2 teaspoons whole cloves

2 teaspoons dill seeds

2 teaspoons small dried whole red chili peppers

I teaspoon whole black peppercorns

Combine all ingredients. Store in a tightly sealed container.

CURRY SPICE MIX

There are many different curry blends on the market. You can make your own custom blend easily. Begin with our mix and vary the chili powder and pepper according to the level of hotness you prefer. Other spices, including the mustard, can be adjusted to suit your tastes.

YIELD: ABOUT ⅓ CUP

4 teaspoons ground coriander

2 teaspoons ground cumin

2 teaspoons ground turmeric

I teaspoon ground ginger

I teaspoon ground cinnamon

I teaspoon ground fenugreek

½ teaspoon chili powder

¼ teaspoon ground cloves

¼ teaspoon dry powdered mustard

¼ teaspoon ground black pepper

Combine all spices well. Store in an airtight jar.

Mustard was known to be an ingredient in Indian curry thousands of years ago.

*"A number of chaps down there
as warm as mustard
about going to war."*

SEBA SMITH ON MAJOR JACK DOWNING

APPETIZERS

SHRIMP & SNOW PEAS

What a treat — real taste and no fat! An elegant but simple presentation for an appetizer. Wonderful served with Currant Sauce.   YIELD: 36 APPETIZERS

36 snow peas

36 medium shrimp, peeled

Bring a pot of water to a boil. Place the peas in the pot and blanch for 45 seconds after the water returns to a boil. Immediately remove from water with a slotted spoon and rinse them under cold water; drain. Remove string from peas.

Place shrimp in the cooking water and boil for 2 to 3 minutes, or until pink. Drain and rinse with cold water.

Wrap a pea pod around a shrimp and secure with a toothpick; repeat. Arrange and serve with sauce.

1 APPETIZER = 15 CALORIES; 3 GRAMS PROTEIN; 0 GRAMS FAT; 19 MGS. CHOLESTEROL; 19 MGS. SODIUM

QUICK MUSTARD DIP

Need a great tasting dip in a hurry? Open a jar of one of your favorite flavored mustards and serve as is or stir in a tablespoon or two into sour cream.

Skinny Quick Mustard Dip

Just substitute non-fat or light sour cream for regular. Mustard is naturally low in calories.

 # SHRIMP REMOULADE

Outstanding as an appetizer or a salad.   SERVES 8 AS A SALAD

1½ pounds shrimp
2 tablespoons wine vinegar
½ cup light mayonnaise
1 celery rib, minced
3 tablespoons Lemon, Lime or Lemon-Lime mustard
1 tablespoon tarragon or white wine vinegar
salt and pepper
1 teaspoon paprika
1 teaspoon seafood seasoning
⅛ teaspoon cayenne
lettuce, red leaf preferred

Sauté shrimp in 2 tablespoons wine vinegar. Next combine all remaining ingredients, except lettuce. Fold in shrimp.

Chill covered overnight in refrigerator. Pile into a lettuce-lined bowl or on individual plates. (Red lettuce makes a beautiful presentation.)

3-OUNCE SERVING = 113 CALORIES; 18 GRAMS PROTEIN; 2 GRAMS FAT; 134 MGS. CHOLESTEROL; 175 MGS. SODIUM

COOKING WITH MUSTARDS · Appetizers

 **BEEF TERIYAKI**

Prepare and marinate ahead so flavors will blend.   YIELD: 18 APPETIZERS

⅔ cup pineapple juice

½ cup light soy sauce

¼ cup dry sherry

2 tablespoons packed brown sugar

1 tablespoon Dijon-style or Sweet 'N' Hot mustard

4 cloves garlic, minced

2 teaspoons dry mustard

1 ½ pounds beef tenderloin, partially frozen

Combine all ingredients except meat. Set marinade aside. Cut the partially frozen meat into thin strips and complete thawing. Add meat to marinade. Marinate overnight. Thread meat accordion-style onto bamboo skewers. Grill over hot coals to desired doneness, about 5 to 7 minutes. Turn and baste with marinade frequently.

3-OUNCE SERVING = 158 CALORIES; 25 GRAMS PROTEIN; 5.7 GRAMS FAT; 70 MGS. CHOLESTEROL; 39 MGS. SODIUM

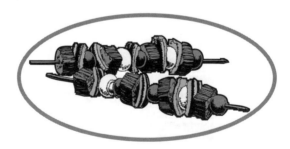

You may cook with dry or prepared mustards — each has its own character and flavor.

BEER AND CHEESE SPREAD

What a combination! Taste variations are in the choice of mustard used. Try this melted over taco chips or baked potatoes, plain or with broccoli. If you have a food processor, this recipe is a snap.   YIELD: ABOUT 3 CUPS

I pound sharp Cheddar cheese, shredded

I pound Swiss cheese, shredded

I teaspoon Worcestershire sauce

2 tablespoons English Pub, Jalapeño or Hot Swedish-Style mustard

I teaspoon dry mustard

I clove garlic, minced

1/2 to 2/3 cup flat beer

Bring cheeses to room temperature. Combine cheeses, Worcestershire sauce, mustards and garlic. Beat in enough beer to make a spreading consistency.

1/2 CUP SERVING = 595 CALORIES; 40 GRAMS PROTEIN; 45 GRAMS FAT; 147 MGS. CHOLESTEROL; 659 MGS. SODIUM

LIGHT BEER AND CHEESE SPREAD

Make as directed but substitute low-fat Cheddar and Swiss cheeses for these calorie-reducing results:

1/2 CUP SERVING = 275 CALORIES; 37 GRAMS PROTEIN; 11 GRAMS FAT; 53 MG. CHOLESTEROL; 218 MG. SODIUM

NOTE: If preferred, you may substitute light or non-alcoholic beer for traditional beer for additional calorie savings.

"What is special about MFK Fisher is not the tedious stuff about six teaspoons of dry mustard, but the literary dressing around the sides of the recipe."
PHILIP HOWARD

COOKING
WITH
Gourmet
MUSTARDS

SALADS

SALAD DRESSINGS

MAYONNAISE

SOUPS

 ## MARINATED COLE SLAW

Make this a day ahead of serving so the flavors have a chance to blend.

YIELD: 6 SERVINGS

> ½ red cabbage, shredded
> ½ green cabbage, shredded
> I red onion, thinly sliced
> I bell pepper, red or green, chopped
> I carrot, grated
> ¼ cup sugar

Mix all ingredients together in a large bowl; cover. Set aside while making dressing.

Cole Slaw Dressing:

YIELD: ABOUT ½ CUP

> ¼ cup white wine vinegar*
> ¼ cup vegetable oil
> I tablespoon Dijon-style mustard*
> I teaspoon salt
> I teaspoon pepper

Place all ingredients in a saucepan and bring to a boil, stirring frequently. Boil for 3 minutes. Let cool and add to vegetable slaw mixture. Mix well, re-cover and refrigerate overnight.

I SERVING = 144 CALORIES, 0 GM. PROTEIN, 2.3 GM FAT, 0 MGS. CHOLESTEROL, 388 MGS. SODIUM

* If you make your own specialty vinegars, as we do from the book *Gourmet Vinegars* by Marsha Peters Johnson, you can make endless variations of this recipe. Some of our favorites are: Lime Vinegar and Lime Mustard, Apricot Vinegar and Sweet 'N' Hot Mustard, and any Herb Vinegar with matching Herbed Mustard.

LO-CAL PIQUANT SHELL PASTA

This is very tangy when it is first made, however the flavors mellow as it chills. An excellent pasta salad.

YIELD: 8 SERVINGS

Salad:

8 ounces shell pasta, cooked, drained and cooled
3 ribs of celery, chopped
8 green onions, chopped
1 carrot, shredded
1 long green chili, peeled and chopped
1 cup steamed broccoli florets
1 red bell pepper, chopped

Dressing:

1 ½ cups low-fat or regular Italian salad dressing
3 tablespoons Basil, Cilantro, Tarragon or Herbed vinegar
1 tablespoon Basil, Tarragon, Herbes de Provence, Three Herbs, Red Wine, Green Peppercorn or Black Peppercorn mustard
salt and pepper
2 ounces fresh grated Parmesan cheese

Combine pasta, celery, onions, carrot, chili, broccoli and bell pepper in a large bowl. In separate bowl, combine dressing ingredients: Italian dressing, vinegar, mustard and desired amount of salt and pepper. Toss with salad mixture. Adjust seasonings and chill before serving. Grate cheese over salad before serving.

1 SERVING = 154 CALORIES; 7.5 GRAMS PROTEIN; 2.9 GRAMS FAT; 6.5 MGS. CHOLESTEROL; 272 MGS. SODIUM

"The embarrassing thing is that the salad dressing is out-grossing my films."
PAUL NEWMAN

EGGLESS EGG SALAD

A healthy eggless substitute for classic egg salad that uses tofu as its base. Mustard is the key ingredient for flavor and paired with turmeric makes the salad yellow. It's hard to tell the difference and makes healthy sandwiches. YIELD: ABOUT 1 1/2 CUPS

> 1 (12.3-ounce) package or block firm tofu
> 1/4 cup reduced calorie eggless mayonnaise
> 2 teaspoons Dijon-style mustard
> 1/2 teaspoon honey
> 1/4 teaspoon turmeric
> 1/4 teaspoon dry mustard
> 1/8 teaspoon salt
> 1/8 teaspoon pepper
> 1/4 cup (1 stalk) finely chopped celery
> 1 minced green onion or 1 teaspoon dry onion
> 1 tablespoon pickle relish

Drain tofu. Crumble tofu in a medium bowl. Add mayonnaise, Dijon-style mustard, honey, turmeric, dry mustard, salt and pepper, stirring to combine well. Stir in celery, onion and pickle relish. Cover and refrigerate at least an hour to let flavors blend before serving.

1 SERVING (2 TABLESPOONS) = 30 CALORIES; 3 GRAMS PROTEIN; 1 GRAM FAT; 0 MG. CHOLESTEROL; 120 MGS. SODIUM

The next time you make a mixed greens salad, add mustard sprouts to the mixture. It adds that spicy nip that mustard is famous for, in a new way.

Optional Add-ins to <u>Eggless Egg Salad</u>

Add any or all of the following to suit your taste:

2 tablespoons chopped tomatoes

1 tablespoon chopped green pepper

1 teaspoon minced fresh parsley or ½ teaspoon dried

1 teaspoon minced capers

¼ teaspoon dill weed

HONEY MUSTARD MAYONNAISE

Perfect on ham, chicken or turkey sandwiches. Serve it with meats, cold cuts, chicken or vegetables as compliments.   YIELD: ABOUT 1¼ CUPS

1 cup prepared or home-made mayonnaise

3 tablespoons Honey-Dijon mustard

1 tablespoon coarse-grain mustard such as Bavarian Brown

2 teaspoons lemon juice

Combine all ingredients, whisk until completely blended. Let flavors blend for at least 30 minutes in refrigerator before serving. Store in refrigerator.

MUSTARD MAYONNAISE

Make this quickly in your food processor or blender. Add oil very slowly to egg mixture until it begins to thicken. If you do not wish to use a fresh egg, coddle it first for 1 minute.

YIELD: 1¾ CUPS

1 egg, at room temperature
1½ teaspoons dry mustard
½ teaspoon salt
¼ teaspoon white pepper or dash of cayenne
¼ cup olive or vegetable oil, at room temperature
1 cup vegetable oil, at room temperature
2 tablespoons lemon juice
3 tablespoons Dijon or coarse-grained mustard

Use metal knife blade in food processor. Add egg, dry mustard, salt and pepper; process for 30 seconds or until fluffy. With machine running, slowly drizzle ¼ cup olive oil through food chute until mixture begins to thicken. Continue adding oil slowly. Add lemon juice and mustard, pulsing to combine. Refrigerate.

Spread one of your favorite gourmet mustards on your next grilled cheese or peanut butter sandwich for a real flavor punch!

PIQUANT MUSTARD SALAD DRESSING

Try this on a spinach salad for raves. Change the mustards and vinegars for tasty variations. YIELD: ABOUT 2 CUPS

 1/4 cup sugar
 3 tablespoons Dijon-style mustard
 1 teaspoon salt, optional
 1/2 teaspoon pepper
 1/2 teaspoon garlic powder
 1 teaspoon Worcestershire sauce
 2 tablespoon lemon juice
 1 cup vegetable oil
 1/2 cup white wine vinegar

Mix all the ingredients, except oil and vinegar, in a small bowl. Add a small amount of the oil to make a paste. Put the remaining oil and vinegar into a blender; add the paste and blend briefly until mixed. Serve.

If you would like a different "French Dip" sandwich, just dip the sandwich into your mustard vinaigrette instead of au jus.

CREAMY MUSTARD SALAD DRESSING

A smooth, creamy dressing that has so many delicious variations. Simply vary the mustard for a new flavor experience.   YIELD: 1/3 CUP

> 1/4 cup light mayonnaise
>
> I tablespoon skim evaporated milk
>
> I tablespoon any Dijon-based mustard, such as Black Peppercorn or Honey mustard
>
> 1/2 teaspoon dry mustard
>
> 1/2 teaspoon salt
>
> 1/8 teaspoon white pepper

In a small bowl, mix all ingredients thoroughly. Chill and serve.

I TABLESPOON = 35 CALORIES; 0 GRAMS PROTEIN, 3.3 GRAMS FAT, 6.6 MGS. CHOLESTEROL, 80 MGS. SODIUM

PARMESAN DRESSING

This flavorful dressing may be prepared just before putting your green salad together. Or try it with an Italian accent, adding garbanzo or kidney beans, sliced Italian salami, cubes of mozzarella cheese and olives for a salad entrée. Toss with dressing and serve.

YIELD: ABOUT 1/2 CUP

> 2 tablespoons white wine vinegar
>
> I teaspoon dry mustard
>
> 1/4 teaspoon salt
>
> 1/4 teaspoon pepper
>
> 1/4 teaspoon sugar
>
> 1/8 teaspoon onion powder
>
> 1/4 cup olive or salad oil
>
> 2 tablespoons grated Parmesan cheese

In a small bowl, add vinegar, mustard, salt, pepper, sugar and onion powder; stir to combine. Add oil and stir until blended. Stir in cheese.

BALSAMIC–MUSTARD VINAIGRETTE

A salad dressing classic. Choose garlic or chives according to your taste. May also be made in the blender or food processor. YIELD: ABOUT 1 CUP

1 tablespoon Dijon-style mustard
4 tablespoons balsamic vinegar
sea salt, to taste
freshly ground black pepper
¾ cup olive oil
1 small clove garlic, finely minced or
 1 teaspoon fresh minced chives

Whisk mustard, vinegar, salt and pepper together. Slowly pour in oil, whisking constantly until all oil has been added and dressing is creamy and thickened. Stir in garlic or chives. Cover and let flavors mingle awhile before serving.

Mustard is an emulsifier. Add enough mustard to a salad dressing and it will help hold the oil and vinegar together. It can also minimize the possibility of curdling when used in a Hollandaise sauce.

HELENE'S POPPYSEED DRESSING

This is Helene's special dressing. It is one of our favorites; try it and see if you agree.

YIELD: ABOUT 1¾ CUPS

½ cup honey
⅓ cup tarragon vinegar
1 teaspoon salt, optional
½ teaspoon dry mustard
2 tablespoons Tarragon Mustard
1 large shallot, minced
1 cup salad oil
1 tablespoon poppyseeds

Combine honey, vinegar, salt, dry mustard, Tarragon Mustard and shallot in blender; blend briefly. Turn blender on low, remove lid and slowly pour oil in a thin and steady stream. Scrape down sides as needed. Turn off blender, add poppy seeds, re-cover and pulse once or twice to mix. Store in refrigerator. Use within 2 weeks.

VARIATIONS of Helene's Poppyseed Dressing

Use Helene's master recipe and change the vinegars and mustards as directed to create these special gourmet dressings:

Aioli Dressing
Omit poppyseeds. Use 1/3 cup white wine vinegar and 2 tablespoons Aioli-Garlic Mustard.

Cranberry Dressing
Omit poppyseeds. Use 1/3 cup red wine vinegar and 2 tablespoons Cranberry Mustard.

Honey Mustard Dressing #1
Omit poppyseeds. Use 1/3 cup of white wine vinegar and 2 tablespoons Honey Mustard.

Honey Mustard Dressing #2
Omit poppyseeds. Use 1/3 cup red wine vinegar and 2 tablespoons Honey Mustard.

Berry Dressing #1
Use 1/3 cup sweet rice wine vinegar and 2 tablespoons Berry Mustard.

Berry Dressing #2
Use 1/3 cup red wine vinegar and 2 tablespoons Berry Mustard.

Peppercorn Dressing
Omit poppyseeds. Use 1/3 cup rice wine vinegar and 2 tablespoons Black Peppercorn Mustard.

Lime Poppyseed Dressing
Use 1/3 cup white wine vinegar and 2 tablespoons Lime Mustard.

CREAM OF MUSTARD SOUP

A superb and unusual soup that is both rich and delicate in flavor. Garnish with onions.

SERVES 6 AS A MAIN COURSE OR 12 AS A SOUP COURSE

2 (12-ounce) cans chicken broth or 24 ounces homemade broth

2 ½ cups white wine, Chablis preferred

2 egg yolks

1 cup heavy cream

white pepper

2 tablespoons butter

1 tablespoons flour

1 tablespoon dry mustard

3 tablespoons Herbes de Provence Mustard

3 green onions, chopped (for garnish)

Pour chicken broth and wine into a saucepan and bring to a boil. Reduce the heat and keep warm over low heat.

In a small bowl, beat the egg yolks with cream and desired amount of pepper; set aside.

In a soup pot, over low heat, melt the butter and whisk in flour and dry mustard to make a roux. Stir for one minute. Slowly pour in the hot chicken broth/wine mixture, whisking until smooth and thickened. Add a little of the thickened chicken broth mixture to the eggs and cream and stir. Pour cream mixture into the soup pot, stirring constantly. Remove pan from the heat; add mustard. Garnish with green onions.

BASED ON 12 SERVINGS, 1 SERVING = 173 CALORIES; 2.7 GRAMS PROTEIN; 10.6 GRAMS FAT; 65.3 MGS. CHOLESTEROL; 160 MGS. SODIUM

VARIATIONS of <u>Cream of Mustard Soup</u>

Substitute different mustards for new flavors:

<u>Lemon Mustard</u>, garnished with a slice of lemon

<u>Lime Mustard</u>, garnished with a slice of lime

<u>Basil Mustard</u>, garnished with a fresh leaf of basil

<u>Dill Mustard</u>, garnished with a sprinkle of dill

<u>Tarragon Mustard</u>, garnished with a few tarragon leaves

<u>Champagne Mustard</u>, garnished with strips of cold chicken breast

<u>Green Peppercorn Mustard</u>, garnished with green peppercorns

<u>Shallot Mustard</u>, garnished with cold baby shrimp

 # LIGHT CREAM OF MUSTARD SOUP

Great taste, but in a lighter mode. SERVES 6 TO 12

2 (12-ounce) cans chicken broth or 24 ounces homemade broth
2½ cups white wine, Chablis preferred
white pepper
1 cup skim evaporated milk
1 tablespoon light margarine or butter
1 tablespoon flour
1 tablespoon Herbes de Provence Mustard
3 green onions, chopped (for garnish)

Follow the directions for <u>Cream of Mustard Soup</u>.

BASED ON 12 SERVINGS = 105 CALORIES EACH; 3.4 GRAMS PROTEIN; 1.7 GRAMS FAT; 24.6 MGS. CHOLESTEROL, 144 MGS. SODIUM

America loves mustard but so do many other countries. In France, known for its love of fine wine, they hold mustard in such high regard that they even age some of their mustards in wooden casks.

EGGS and SEAFOOD

EGGS HELENE

Helene's recipe has been served in a local restaurant to the delight of mustard-loving diners. Try this for a special breakfast or late supper. Two versions are offered, traditional and a lower fat and lower cholesterol recipe.   YIELD: 2 TO 3 SERVINGS

6 eggs
1 tablespoon Herbes de Provence Mustard
salt and pepper
2 tablespoons butter
2 ounces sharp Cheddar cheese, grated

In a bowl, scramble the eggs; add mustard and desired amount of salt and pepper. Melt butter in a sauté pan over low heat. Add the egg mixture and cook to desired doneness. Sprinkle cheese over top; serve.

 EGGS HELENE LIGHT

Great taste in this lighter version too.   YIELD: 2 TO 3 SERVINGS

> 1 cup egg substitute (see following recipe)
> 2 tablespoons Herbes de Provence Mustard
> salt and pepper
> vegetable oil spray
> 2 ounces low-fat sharp Cheddar cheese, grated

In a bowl combine egg substitute, mustard and desired amount of salt and pepper. Spray sauté pan and place over low heat. Add egg mixture and cook to desired doneness. Sprinkle cheese over top; serve.

1 SERVING = 218 CALORIES; 22.3 GRAMS PROTEIN; 9 GRAMS FAT; 13 MGS. CHOLESTEROL; 606 MGS. SODIUM

HOMEMADE EGG SUBSTITUTE

Tastes better than commercial brands and is less expensive to make. May be used in place of eggs when asked for in recipes. (1/4 cup = 1 whole egg)   YIELD: 1 CUP

> 6 egg whites
> 1/4 cup powdered skim milk
> 1 tablespoon vegetable oil

Mix ingredients together until smooth. Store in a jar in the refrigerator up to 1 week. This also freezes well.

1 EGG EQUIVALENT = 81 CALORIES; 7.7 GRAMS PROTEIN; 3.5 GRAMS FAT; 1.5 MGS. CHOLESTEROL; 77.8 MGS. SODIUM

FRITTATA
Italian-Style Baked Omelette

This is wonderful! Present with the sauce and Italian sausage.   YIELD: 6 SERVINGS

½ cup broccoli florets

20 Chinese snow peas, trimmed

3 green onions, 1-inch diagonally cut

9 eggs or equivalent egg substitute

4 tablespoons Herbes de Provence Mustard

1 teaspoon dry mustard

3 tablespoons butter

1 (6-ounce) jar marinated artichoke hearts

6 fresh mushrooms, thickly sliced

Preheat the oven to 375°. Steam the broccoli, snow peas and green onions conventionally for 5 minutes or microwave, covered, for 1 minute on High. Set vegetables aside covered.

In a large bowl, scramble eggs with mustards. In an ovenproof skillet, melt butter, then pour in the egg mixture. Next add all vegetables and place skillet in the oven. Bake 45 to 55 minutes, uncovered, until the eggs have set in the middle. Make the sauce while the eggs are baking (see recipe following).

1 SERVING = 192 CALORIES; 9.8 GRAMS PROTEIN; 16.8 GRAMS FAT; 428 MGS. CHOLESTEROL; 165 MGS. SODIUM

 NOTE: You will greatly reduce the cholesterol and fat content if you use egg substitute instead of eggs.

FRITTATA SAUCE

This is the real thing — rich and wonderful.

> 3 egg yolks or equivalent egg substitute
> ¼ pound (1 stick) unsalted butter, cut into 16 pats
> 1 cup grated Swiss cheese
> 2 tablespoons Herbes de Provence Mustard

Place egg yolks in the top of a double boiler, over simmering — not boiling — water. Whisk constantly until lemon-colored and thickened. Be sure the heat is not too high, as the yolks will curdle.

Add butter, 2 pats at a time, whisking until melted. Add cheese, a quarter cup at a time, stirring until melted, then add the mustard. Remove from heat and pour over the frittata.

1/6 OF SAUCE = 315 CALORIES; 13.6 GRAMS PROTEIN; 29.5 GRAMS FAT; 215 MGS. CHOLESTEROL; 265 MGS. SODIUM

 NOTE: A low-fat alternative would be to top the frittata with salsa and low-fat grated Cheddar cheese.

1 OUNCE LOW-FAT CHEESE = 50 CALORIES; 7 GRAMS PROTEIN; 2 GRAMS FAT; 10 MGS. CHOLESTEROL; 440 MGS. SODIUM

HERBED SAUSAGE QUICHE

The robust flavor of this company-perfect quiche hides its low-fat and cholesterol count.

YIELD: 8 SERVINGS

vegetable oil spray
3 Italian sausages, slipped out of their casing
1 large shallot, minced
2 red potatoes, sliced thin
9 egg whites
2 eggs
1/4 cup Herbes de Provence Mustard
1/2 teaspoon dry mustard
1 cup skim evaporated milk
2 ounces part skim mozzarella cheese, grated
2 ounces low-fat Cheddar cheese, grated
1 teaspoon baking powder
1/2 teaspoon white pepper

Preheat the oven to 425°. Spray sauté pan with vegetable oil and bring it up to medium heat. Add sausage and shallot. Break sausage up into smaller pieces and sauté until the sausage is cooked through, about 3 to 5 minutes. Drain fat from pan, when cooled wipe out with paper towels. Place sausages on a paper towel and pat to remove as much of the drippings as possible. Set aside.

Spray the sauté pan again and gently sauté the potato slices until they are almost transparent, about 5 minutes. Line the bottom and sides of a 10-inch deep dish baking pan, overlapping the slices to create a shell for the quiche.

Beat the egg whites in a large bowl until frothy. In a medium bowl, combine 2 eggs, mustards, milk, cheeses, baking powder and pepper. Gently stir this mixture into the beaten egg whites.

76   COOKING WITH MUSTARDS • Eggs and Seafood

Arrange the sausage and shallot mixture evenly over the bottom of the potato shell. Pour the egg white mixture over the sausage. Bake 15 minutes. Reduce oven temperature to 300° and continue baking until puffed and golden brown, about 40 minutes. Let cool on a metal rack 10 minutes before slicing. Serve hot.

¹/8 SERVING = 193 CALORIES; 15.1 GRAMS PROTEIN; 9.6 GRAMS FAT; 96.5 MGS. CHOLESTEROL; 471 MGS. SODIUM

 NOTE: Using chicken or turkey Italian-style sausage will reduce cholesterol, fat and calories.

When making your favorite quiche, spread a thin layer of flavored Dijon-style mustard on the crust before filling. It will help prevent a soggy crust and add a zippy flavor.

 # DILLED ALBACORE QUICHE

A great quiche for a luncheon or dinner that is flavorful, hearty and low-fat.

YIELD: 8 SERVINGS

vegetable oil spray

2 red potatoes, sliced thin

2 (7-ounce) cans of water pack albacore tuna, reserve liquid

1 egg, beaten

2 egg whites, beaten

½ cup no-fat or light sour cream

3 tablespoons light mayonnaise

2 tablespoons Dill, Herbes de Provence, Shallot,
   Jalapeño, Lemon, Lime or Black Peppercorn mustard

3 dashes of cayenne

4 ounces low-fat Swiss cheese, grated

2 tablespoons finely chopped green onion

2 large dill pickles, finely chopped

½ teaspoon dried dill weed

Preheat the oven to 325°. Spray a sauté pan with vegetable oil and bring up to medium heat. Sauté potato slices until almost transparent, about 5 minutes.

Line the bottom of a 10-inch deep baking dish with the potatoes, overlapping slices to create a shell for the quiche.

Add water, if necessary, to reserved albacore liquid to make ¼ cup. Pour into a large bowl, stir in the beaten egg and egg whites, sour cream, mayonnaise, mustard and cayenne. Add albacore tuna. Blend in cheese, onion, pickle and dill weed. Pour mixture into potato shell. Bake until set, about 40 minutes. Let cool 10 minutes before slicing.

⅛ SERVING = 161 CALORIES; 17.6 GRAMS PROTEIN; 4.7 GRAMS FAT; 63.8 MGS. CHOLESTEROL, 787 MGS. SODIUM

 ## CHILI RELLENOS QUICHE

Wonderful Mexican food flavors without the high fat calories. The potato shell saves a bunch, so do the egg whites and evaporated milk ... Olé!   YIELD: 8 SERVINGS

- 2 red potatoes, sliced thin
- 9 egg whites
- 2 eggs
- 3 tablespoons Jalapeño Mustard
- 1/2 teaspoons dry mustard
- 1 cup skim evaporated milk
- 2 ounces part skim mozzarella cheese, grated
- 2 ounces low-fat Cheddar cheese, grated
- 1 teaspoon baking powder
- 1 cup cooked chicken breast, diced
- 1 (4-ounce) can chopped green chilies
- 1 large shallot, minced
- 1 teaspoon white pepper
- salsa, for garnish

Preheat oven to 425°. Spray a sauté pan with vegetable oil, bring up to medium heat. Sauté the potato slices until almost transparent, about 5 minutes. Line the bottom of a 10-inch deep baking dish with the potatoes, overlapping slices to create a shell for the quiche.

Beat egg whites in a large bowl until frothy. In medium bowl combine 2 eggs, mustards, milk, cheeses and baking powder. Gently stir mixture into beaten egg whites. Sprinkle chicken, chilies and shallot over the bottom of the potato shell. Pour egg white mixture over chicken. Bake 15 minutes. Reduce oven to 300°. Bake until puffed and golden brown, or about 30 minutes. Garnish with salsa.

1/8 SERVING = 145 CALORIES; 15.4 GRAMS PROTEIN; 4.3 GRAMS FAT; 90.5 GRAMS CHOLESTEROL; 377.6 MGS. SODIUM

 ## SEAFOOD BROIL WITH MUSTARD SAUCE

A recipe that is worth repeating. Your choice of fresh fish makes this a delicious, easy-to-do recipe.
YIELD: 4 SERVINGS

2 teaspoons butter

2 tablespoons minced shallots

1 pound halibut, cod or salmon, steaks or filets

⅛ teaspoon lemon herb seasoning

⅛ teaspoon white pepper

2 tablespoons light mayonnaise

½ cup white wine

1 tablespoon Lemon, Lemon-Lime, Lime, Black Peppercorn or Honey mustard

2 tablespoons chopped fresh parsley

Melt butter and sauté shallots in a small saucepan until transparent. Spread evenly over bottom of broiler-proof baking dish. Place fish in a single layer over shallots.

In a small bowl, combine mayonnaise, lemon seasoning and pepper; spread over fish. Broil 3 inches from heat until fish flakes easily, about 8 to 10 minutes.

Transfer fish to a serving platter. Add baking dish drippings to sauté pan. Add wine and cook over high heat until liquid is reduced by half. Add mustard and parsley, stir and pour over fish. Serve.

EACH 4-OUNCE SERVING:

COD = 163 CALORIES; 25.9 GRAMS PROTEIN; 5.4 GRAMS FAT; 67.7 MGS. CHOLESTEROL; 223 MGS. SODIUM

HALIBUT = 203 CALORIES; 30.3 GRAMS PROTEIN; 7.7 GRAMS FAT; 51.7 MGS. CHOLESTEROL; 214 MGS. SODIUM

SALMON = 254 CALORIES; 31.1 GRAMS PROTEIN; 12.9 GRAMS FAT; 61 MGS. CHOLESTEROL; 202 MGS. SODIUM

 # IMPRESSIVE CRAB

An absolutely elegant entrée. Serve with a crisp mixed greens salad with a salad dressing from this book, warm sourdough bread and a favorite wine.   SERVES 8

    1 green pepper, minced
    1 medium onion, minced
    1 teaspoon dry mustard
    2 tablespoons Herbes de Provence, Horseradish Lovers,
       Black Peppercorn or Lime mustard
    1 tablespoon prepared horseradish
    1 teaspoon white pepper
    1 egg, beaten
    2 egg whites, beaten
    1 cup light mayonnaise
    1 ½ pounds real or imitation crab meat
    4 ounces low-fat Swiss cheese, grated

Preheat the oven to 350°. Combine green pepper, onion, mustards, horseradish, white pepper and eggs; mix well. Blend in mayonnaise, then crab meat. Spoon mixture evenly into individual ovenproof serving dishes. Sprinkle with cheese.

   Arrange dishes on baking pan and bake for 20 minutes until heated through and the cheese is browned.

1 SERVING = 227 CALORIES; 21.8 GRAMS PROTEIN; 13.1 GRAMS FAT; 104.3 MGS. CHOLESTEROL; 135 MGS. SODIUM

SHRIMP DIJON

A rich and creamy Dijonnaise entrée that's absolutely delicious but low in fat and cholesterol. Try it served with lightly sautéed fresh seasonal vegetables and cheese breadsticks.   SERVES 4

    3 tablespoons butter or margarine
    4 tablespoons flour
    2 cups evaporated skim milk
    3 tablespoons Lime, Lemon-Lime, Shallot, Honey or Black
        Peppercorn mustard
    1/2 teaspoon dry mustard
    1/8 teaspoon cayenne
    3 tablespoons minced shallots
    1/2 cup white wine
    1/4 cup parsley, minced
    I egg yolk, beaten
    I pound large shrimp, washed, shelled and deveined
    1/2 cup white wine vinegar
    2 ounces Parmesan cheese, grated

Preheat oven to 450°. Over medium heat melt margarine in a saucepan; stir in flour to make a roux. Reduce heat to low and stir for several minutes. Gradually add milk, stirring constantly, until thickened. Add mustards and cayenne, simmer 10 minutes, stirring occasionally.

Add shallots, wine and parsley; simmer 10 minutes, stirring occasionally. Add 2 tablespoons of this sauce to beaten egg yolk, stirring quickly. Then add egg mixture to remainder of sauce while stirring.

Sauté the shrimp in the vinegar until they turn pink, about 3 minutes. Remove the shrimp from the pan, pour out the vinegar and replace the shrimp in

---

the pan. Add about a third of the sauce; mix.

Spoon into individual ovenproof dishes, cover with the remaining sauce and sprinkle with cheese

Bake 15 minutes or until the cheese turns a golden brown. Serve immediately.

CURRY MUSTARD FISH FILLETS

A quick, easy, low-fat, salt-free and tasty entrée.   SERVES 4

> 2 pounds rockfish fillets
> juice of half a lemon
> 1 tablespoon prepared mustard of choice
> 1/4 teaspoon curry powder
> vegetable oil spray

Preheat oven to 400°. Squeeze lemon juice over fillets. Combine mustard and curry powder. Spread mixture over top of fillets. Place fillets in a pan coated with vegetable oil spray. Bake for 10 minutes, check for doneness. Add additional minutes if necessary. Serve.

7-OUNCE SERVING = 200 CALORIES; 35 GRAMS PROTEIN; 4.8 GRAMS FAT; 160 MGS. CHOLESTEROL; 150 MGS. SODIUM

" … the seed of mustarde pounded with vinegar is an excellent
sauce, good to be eaten with any grosse meates, either fish or
flesh, because it doth help digestion, warmeth the stomache
and provoketh appetite."

JOHN GERARD

"After meat comes mustard … "

MIGUEL DE CERVANTES

BEEF, PORK and POULTRY

POULET MOUTARDE DIJONNAISE HELENE

A simple and expandable recipe done in the French manner. Use any of the Dijon-style mustards in this book. This is a good dinner choice for company.

> chicken pieces of choice
> cooking oil of choice
> any Dijon-style mustard
> dry white wine
> fresh bread crumbs

Brush the chicken pieces with oil and broil on each side.

Combine equal parts of mustard and wine. Brush the chicken with the mustard mixture and sprinkle with bread crumbs. Broil until browned. Serve immediately.

NOTE: To avoid over-browning, cook chicken in microwave until it is half done. Then broil to finish.

The word 'moutard' may be used on French mustard labels only if the mustard is made with black mustard seed.

HONEY-LEMON GLAZED CHICKEN

Quick, easy, low-fat, light and piquant. Nice served with a rice pilaf and garden salad for a fresh, quick and healthy meal.   SERVES 4

> juice of one lemon
> 1/4 cup honey
> 3/4 teaspoon salt
> 1/2 teaspoon dry mustard
> grated peel of one lemon
> 2 tablespoons Lemon, Hot Swedish-Style, Sweet 'N' Hot, Lemon Thyme, Honey Dijon or Shallot mustard
> 4 chicken breasts

Preheat oven to 350°. In a small saucepan, mix all ingredients except chicken over low heat; stir. When well combined and heated, remove from heat. Let cool slightly.

Dip chicken into cooled glaze sauce. Pour remaining sauce over chicken and bake for 45 minutes. Turn chicken over and bake for another 15 minutes.

1 SERVING = 240 CALORIES; 27 GRAMS PROTEIN; 3.1 GRAMS FAT; 73 MG. CHOLESTEROL; 66 MGS. SODIUM

VARIATIONS of Honey-Lemon Glazed Chicken

Honey-Orange Glazed

Omit lemon juice and peel. Substitute: juice of 1/2 orange and grated peel of 1/2 orange. Use Orange Mustard.

Fruited Honey Glazed

Omit lemon juice and peel. Substitute: 1/2 cup crushed pineapple and 1 teaspoon Worcestershire sauce. Use Apricot Mustard.

 ## CHICKEN TARRAGON

The flavors are superb in this company-perfect dish. Entertain in style with this low-fat entrée. Serve with a warm rustic Basque or Tuscan bread to catch every drop of sauce.

SERVES 8

vegetable oil spray

1 pound fresh mushrooms, washed and sliced

8 chicken breasts, skinned and boned

6 shallots, peeled and chopped

2 carrots, sliced in ½-inch rounds

¼ cup brandy or cognac

¼ cup dry white wine

¼ cup fresh tarragon or 2 tablespoons dried tarragon leaves

1 ½ tablespoons chopped fresh chervil or ½ teaspoon dried

1 teaspoon salt

1 teaspoon white pepper

1 cup evaporated skim milk

3 tablespoon Tarragon Mustard

1 egg yolk

1 tablespoon flour

Spray the bottom of a dutch oven or large saucepan with vegetable coating. Sauté mushrooms until tender, remove from pan, leaving the drippings, and set aside. Next, sauté the chicken, about 4 minutes each side. Set chicken aside.

Add shallots and carrots to the drippings in the pan, sauté 5 minutes. Return chicken to pan; add brandy, wine, tarragon, chervil, salt and pepper. Bring to a boil then reduce heat, simmering covered, for 30 minutes.

In a small bowl, combine milk, mustard, egg yolk and flour. Remove chicken to a heated platter to keep warm. Strain drippings in pan, discarding solids.

Return drippings to pan. Mix milk mixture into drippings. Cook over medium heat, adding a little wine if the sauce seems too thick. Return mushrooms to the sauce for 2 minutes before spooning over chicken. Serve.

1 CHICKEN BREAST SERVING = 361 CALORIES; 29.7 GRAMS PROTEIN; 3.9 GRAMS FAT; 109.3 MGS. CHOLESTEROL; 69.5 MGS. SODIUM

VARIATIONS of Chicken Tarragon

Dilled Chicken

Omit tarragon and chervil. Use fresh dill or 2 tablespoons dried dill weed. Replace Tarragon Mustard with Dill Herbed Mustard or Champagne Dill Mustard.

Chicken Olé

Omit shallots, tarragon and chervil. Substitute 1 medium onion, chopped, for shallots. Use fresh cilantro and 1 tablespoon chopped jalapeño. Replace Tarragon Mustard with Jalapeño Mustard.

Cranberry Chicken

Omit tarragon and chervil. Substitute fresh parsley. Replace Tarragon Mustard with Cranberry Mustard.

OMAHA CHICKEN

We doubt that Omaha ever heard of this dish. It was nicknamed by Helene's friend, Robert, and it has stuck. This is a favorite chicken dish so be sure and give it a try. Good with fresh steamed asparagus.   SERVES 4 AS A DINNER ENTRÉE OR 8 AS A LIGHTER COURSE

4 chicken breasts, skinned and boned

1 cup flour

1 teaspoon dry mustard

1 teaspoon white pepper

vegetable oil spray

Lime, Lemon-Lime, Champagne, Champagne Dill, Champagne Shallot, Black Peppercorn, Honey or Apricot mustard

8 thin 2 x 4-inch slices prosciutto ham

8 thin 2 x 4-inch slices Bel Paese or Fontina cheese

¼ cup freshly grated Parmesan cheese

Preheat oven to 350°. Slice breasts horizontally to make 8 thin slices.

In a shallow bowl combine flour, dry mustard and pepper; set aside.

Lay chicken strips on a piece of wax paper. Cover with another piece of wax paper. Pound chicken lightly to flatten pieces. Remove wax paper. Dredge chicken strips through flour mixture, shaking off excess.

Spray vegetable coating into sauté pan. Sauté chicken strips over medium heat until golden brown.

Place chicken in a single layer in baking dish. Brush a thin coat of your mustard choice on each piece. Top with prosciutto ham and cheese slices. Sprinkle with Parmesan. Bake 10 minutes, uncovered, until the cheese melts and is lightly browned.

FOR 4, 1 SERVING = 320 CALORIES; 40.3 GRAMS PROTEIN; 16.2 GRAMS FAT; 117.5 MGS. CHOLESTEROL; 740.8 MGS. SODIUM

FOR 8, 1 SERVING = 160 CALORIES; 20.4 GRAMS PROTEIN; 8.1 GRAMS FAT; 58.8 MGS. CHOLESTEROL; 370.4 MGS. SODIUM

 # LEMON CHICKEN

This dish goes together quickly for busy days. Tastes great and is a low-calorie, low-fat and low-sodium entrée. Sauté small whole mushrooms seasoned with just a dash of garlic powder for a superb accompaniment.   SERVES 4

> 1 teaspoon lemon herb seasoning
> juice of 1/2 fresh lemon
> grated peel of 1/2 lemon
> 2 tablespoons Lemon Mustard
> 1/2 teaspoon white pepper
> 4 skinned chicken breasts (about 1 pound total)

Preheat oven to 350°. Place chicken in a baking dish. Combine lemon herb seasoning, lemon juice, lemon peel, Lemon Mustard and pepper in a small bowl. Pour mixture over chicken. Bake 1 hour. Serve hot.

1 SERVING = 142 CALORIES; 26.7 GRAMS PROTEIN; 3.1 GRAMS FAT; 73 MGS. CHOLESTEROL; 63 MGS. SODIUM

"Tis ever thus with simple folk —
an accepted wit has but to say 'Pass the mustard',
and they roar their ribs out!"
SIR WILLIAM SCHWENCH GILBERT

 ## BARBECUED CHICKEN

Enjoy barbecued chicken without feeling guilty for eating too much fat with this spicy recipe. Team it with vegetable kabobs on the grill and hot corn-on-the-cob to make it a feast!   SERVES 8

vegetable oil spray
1 cup onions, chopped
2 cloves of garlic, minced
1 cup fresh chopped mushrooms
2 tablespoons red wine vinegar
2 tablespoons honey
1/4 cup fresh lime juice
grated peel of one lime
3 tablespoons Lime or Honey mustard
1 1/2 teaspoons pepper
1 teaspoon salt
1/4 cup light soy sauce
2/3 cup red wine
1/2 cup chili sauce
8 chicken breasts, skinned and boned

Spray sauté pan with vegetable spray. Sauté onions, garlic and mushrooms until tender. Add remaining ingredients, except chicken, mix well. Baste chicken breasts with mixture.

Barbecue on a hot grill until done, about 30 minutes per side. They may also be cooked in a preheated 350° oven for 1 hour. Baste frequently with either method.

1 SERVING = 210 CALORIES; 29.2 GRAMS PROTEIN; 3.2 GRAMS FAT; 73 MG. CHOLESTEROL; 425 MG. SODIUM

 # MARINATED CHICKEN

This is perfect hot weather fare. Start the barbecue and enjoy this light and low-calorie entrée. Foil wrapped potatoes roasted in the hot coals work well with the cooking time in this recipe. Chicken may be baked if preferred. SERVES 4

½ cup soy sauce

½ cup raspberry vinegar or other vinegar of choice

½ cup red wine, optional

2 tablespoons fresh grated ginger

2 cloves garlic, pressed

2 tablespoons any Dijon-style mustard

½ teaspoon curry

I tablespoon dry mustard

4 skinned, boneless chicken breasts (about I pound)

Combine soy sauce, vinegar, wine, ginger, garlic, Dijon-style mustard, curry and dry mustard in a large bowl. Place the chicken in the marinade mixture, coating well; cover and marinate for 6 hours or more.

Barbecue on hot coals for 30 minutes per side or bake in a preheated 350° oven for I hour.

I SERVING = 142 CALORIES; 26.7 GRAMS PROTEIN; 3.1 GRAMS FAT; 73 MGS. CHOLESTEROL; 63 MGS. SODIUM

MARINATED PORK MEDALLIONS
With Cranberry Mustard Sauce

This may become one of your favorite pork recipes too. Very festive for the holidays.

SERVES 4

I pound pork tenderloin, cut into ¾-inch medallions

salt

pepper

½ cup Cranberry, Honey, Lemon, Lime, Apricot,
  Hot Swedish-Style, Champagne or Orange mustard

I cup red wine vinegar

Sauce:

vegetable oil spray

¼ cup minced shallots

2 tablespoons flour

2 tablespoons chicken broth

3 tablespoons whole cranberry sauce

I tablespoon chopped parsley

Place medallions in a shallow dish. Season with salt and pepper. Mix mustard and vinegar; pour over medallions. Cover and marinate in refrigerator overnight.

Preheat oven to 425°. Remove medallions from marinade. Spray sauté pan with vegetable oil, brown medallions over medium heat, remove, and sauté shallots. Stir in flour and chicken broth. When thickened, add cranberry sauce and parsley. Pour mixture over medallions and bake for 20 minutes.

I (4-OUNCE) SERVING = 230 CALORIES; 32.7 GRAMS PROTEIN; 5.5 GRAMS FAT; 105.3 MGS. CHOLESTEROL; 79 MGS. SODIUM

SPARERIBS YOU WON'T FORGET

This is a summertime favorite. Easy to make for hot weather cooking or try them in the oven in mid-winter. SERVES 8

vegetable oil spray
1 cup chopped onions
2 garlic cloves, chopped
1 cup fresh sliced or minced mushrooms
2 tablespoons red wine vinegar
2 tablespoons honey
1/4 cup lime juice
grated peel of one lime
3 tablespoons Lime Mustard
2 teaspoons pepper
1 teaspoon salt
1/4 cup light soy sauce
2/3 cup red wine
1/2 cup chili sauce
2 pounds spareribs, cut into serving size pieces

Spray sauté pan with oil and sauté onion, garlic and mushrooms until tender. Add remaining ingredients, mix well. Baste spareribs with mixture. Barbecue on grill, basting with sauce frequently, until done. Spareribs may also be baked in a preheated 325° oven for 1 hour. Baste frequently with either method.

VARIATION

Lemon Herb Ribs
Substitute lemon juice and peel for lime and use any herbed mustard.

They roused him with muffins – they roused him with ice –
They roused him with mustard and cress –
They roused him with jam and judicious advice –
They set him conundrums to guess.

Lewis Carroll

VEGETABLES

LIGHT & CHEESY POTATOES

This is sure to be a favorite. Delicious with grilled fish.　　　SERVES 6

> 3 large cooked potatoes, peeled and cubed
> I tablespoon butter or margarine
> 1/3 cup thinly sliced green onions
> 2 tablespoons flour
> I cup chicken broth
> I teaspoon caraway seed
> 1/2 teaspoon cumin
> salt
> pepper
> 3 tablespoons Herbes de Provence, Hot Swedish-Style or
>　　Sweet 'N' Hot mustard
> I cup shredded low-fat Swiss cheese
> 1/2 cup fresh, coarse bread crumbs
> 1/8 teaspoon paprika

Place cubed potatoes in a 2-quart casserole. In saucepan, melt margarine, add onions and sauté until transparent. Add flour and cook until bubbly. Add broth, caraway, cumin, salt, pepper and mustard. Cook until thickened. Pour sauce over potatoes. Spread cheese on top, sprinkle with bread crumbs and paprika. Bake, uncovered, at 400° for 20 minutes.

1/6 SERVING = 123 CALORIES; 6.6 GRAMS PROTEIN; 3.5 GRAMS FAT; 6.8 MGS. CHOLESTEROL; 405 MGS. SODIUM

SPICY CROWNED VEGETABLE PLATTER

The tangy mustard topping crowns cooked vegetables such as: cauliflower, broccoflower, broccoli or cabbage. Stunning for company or special occasions as a vegetable centerpiece. Surround center vegetable with colorful cooked vegetables such as peas, brussels sprouts, baby carrots, zucchini or green beans. Garnish with tiny tomatoes if desired.

Topping:

> 1/2 cup mayonnaise, regular, light or non-fat
> I teaspoon dry powdered mustard
> I tablespoon fresh minced onion or I 1/2 teaspoons dried
> 1/2 cup shredded cheese, Cheddar or Jalapeño Jack

Prepare topping by combining mayonnaise, mustard and onion. Set aside to allow flavors to blend for at least 15 minutes. Reserve cheese.

Vegetables:

Select cauliflower or other large vegetable. Wash and cut off leaves and stems, leaving whole. Steam or microwave. Cook smaller vegetables separately.

To microwave: Wrap whole cauliflower in plastic wrap or double wrap in waxed paper, tucking ends underneath. Prick plastic wrap for steam vents. Microwave on High at 8 minutes per pound. Let sit, covered, 5 to 10 minutes.

When small vegetables have been cooked, remove wrap from large vegetable and place on platter. Put topping on crown. Sprinkle shredded cheese over topping. Microwave for I to I 1/2 minutes, or place under broiler, until cheese melts a little. Place hot smaller vegetables around centerpiece. Serve hot. Slice center vegetable in pie-shaped wedges to include topping for each serving.

⊙ SESAME BROCCOLI

Serve this with Marinated Chicken for a light, Oriental-style meal under 250 calories per serving.   SERVES 4

    1 pound cooked broccoli spears
    1 tablespoon salad oil
    1 tablespoon vinegar, any flavor
    1 tablespoon soy sauce
    1 tablespoon any Dijon-style mustard
    4 teaspoons sugar
    1 tablespoon toasted sesame seeds

Place cooked broccoli in a serving dish. Combine all remaining ingredients in a saucepan. Stir and bring to a boil. Pour over spears, turn gently to coat evenly. Serve.

1 SERVING = 50 CALORIES; 2 GRAMS FAT; 174 MGS. SODIUM

Mix in a bit of any flavored Dijon-style mustard, to taste, in your favorite potato salad recipe. A great flavor pick-up!

VEGETABLE VINAIGRETTE

*Need something a little extraordinaire? Try this with asparagus or leeks. Just as good
served cold as hot. Vinaigrette may be made up to a week in advance.* SERVES 6

> 2 cups dry white wine
> 3 whole cloves
> I pound fresh vegetable

Vinaigrette:

> 2 tablespoons Tarragon, Hot Swedish-Style or Champagne
> mustard
> I teaspoon salt
> ½ teaspoon fresh pepper
> ¼ teaspoon sugar
> ¼ cup tarragon vinegar or apple cider vinegar
> ½ cup vegetable oil
> 2 tablespoons fresh or I tablespoon dried tarragon or parsley

Combine wine and cloves in a saucepan, bring to a boil. Add fresh vegetable,
reduce heat and poach gently until tender. Drain, transfer to a shallow bowl,
cover and refrigerate (if serving cold).

Prepare vinaigrette by combining mustard, salt, pepper and sugar in a blender.
Add vinegar and continue to blend. Add oil in a steady stream while blending.
When liquid has thickened, add tarragon and mix 3 to 4 seconds more.

To serve, arrange vegetables in a small shallow dish and pour vinaigrette
over.

I TABLESPOON SERVING = 50 CALORIES; 2 GRAMS FAT; I74 MGS. SODIUM

LIGHT ITALIAN TOMATOES

A festive and tasty topping for tomatoes.   SERVES 8

4 large tomatoes, cut in half
pinch of salt
1 tablespoon any herbed mustard
1 tablespoon chopped shallot or green onion
2 tablespoons chopped green pepper
1 tablespoon chopped fresh basil or ½ tablespoon dried
2 ounces grated Parmesan cheese

Preheat oven to 425°. Place tomatoes, cut side up in a baking dish. Sprinkle with salt. Spread cut side of tomatoes with mustard. Combine shallot, green pepper and basil; spoon onto tomatoes. Sprinkle with Parmesan cheese. Bake for 10 minutes or until cheese turns golden brown.

HALF TOMATO = 44 CALORIES: 3.4 GRAMS PROTEIN; 2.2 GRAMS FAT; 5.5MGS. CHOLESTEROL; 135 MGS. SODIUM

If you are cooking with dry mustard, be aware that it is similar to curry in hotness.

HOT STUFFED ARTICHOKES

An elegant, sizzling side dish or appetizer.

SERVES 4 TO 6 AS A SIDE DISH

½ cup low-calorie Italian salad dressing
1 tablespoon Herbes de Provence or any herbed mustard
⅛ teaspoon garlic powder
1 (14-ounce) can artichoke bottoms, drained
¼ pound part-skim mozzarella cheese, cut in ½-inch cubes
6 slices 95% fat-free ham, cut into strips

Preheat oven to 350°. Drain artichokes. Combine dressing, mustard and garlic powder. Add artichokes to mixture; marinate 4 to 6 hours.

Place cheese in well of artichoke bottom; wrap with ham strip and secure with wooden toothpick. Place on baking pan and bake about 15 minutes or until cheese is melted and artichoke is hot. Serve warm.

1 ARTICHOKE BOTTOM = 27 CALORIES; 2 GRAMS PROTEIN; 1.5 GRAMS FAT; 4 MGS. CHOLESTEROL; 129 MGS. SODIUM

"We believe that mustard bites the tongue,
that pepper is hot, friction-matches incendiary,
revolvers are to be avoided and
suspenders hold up pantaloons."

RALPH WALDO EMERSON

DESSERTS

Mustard is a spice and as such can be used nicely along with cloves, cinnamon or allspice.

HERMITS

This recipe uses mustard as a spice and provides a deliciously different twist to an old-fashioned drop cookie favorite. MAKES ABOUT 4 DOZEN COOKIES

2 ½ cups flour

1 teaspoon baking soda

¼ teaspoon salt

¾ teaspoon allspice

¾ teaspoon cinnamon

½ teaspoon cloves

½ teaspoon dry mustard

½ cup shortening, butter or margarine

1 cup honey

½ cup packed brown sugar

1 teaspoon Hot Swedish-Style Mustard

2 eggs, beaten

3 tablespoon milk

1 cup dried currants

1 cup chopped dates

½ cup chopped walnuts, pecans or hazelnuts

Preheat oven to 400°. Sift together flour, baking soda, salt, allspice, cinnamon, cloves and dry mustard. Set aside.

In a separate large bowl cream shortening, honey, brown sugar and Swedish mustard together. Add eggs to creamed mixture. Alternately add milk and sifted dry ingredients to creamed mixture; mix well. Stir in currants, dates and nuts. Drop from teaspoon onto a lightly greased baking sheet. Bake for 10 to 12 minutes.

SPICED CHOCOLATE CAKE

This has been one of the most popular and requested recipes in this cookbook. Try it and you will see why. This extra-moist cake needs no frosting. Great packed in a lunch box or for a picnic.   MAKES ONE 9 X 13-INCH SHEET CAKE

½ cup butter or margarine, softened
½ cup vegetable oil
1 ¾ cups sugar
2 eggs
1 ½ teaspoons vanilla
½ cup sour milk
1 teaspoon Hot Swedish-Style Mustard
2 ½ cups flour
4 heaping tablespoons cocoa
1 ½ teaspoons baking powder
1 teaspoon cinnamon
1 teaspoon ground cloves
1 teaspoon dry mustard
2 cups zucchini, finely diced or shredded
¾ cup semi-sweet chocolate chips

Preheat oven to 350°. Cream butter, oil and sugar together. Add eggs, vanilla, milk and Swedish mustard to creamed ingredients; combine well with mixer. In a separate bowl combine flour, cocoa, baking powder, cinnamon, cloves and dry mustard; add to the creamed mixture. Stir in zucchini and half of the chocolate chips.

Pour mixture into prepared 9 x 13 x 2-inch baking pan. Sprinkle with remaining chocolate chips. Bake for 40 to 45 minutes or until toothpick comes out clean. Serve warm or cooled.

NOTE: To lower the calories, substitute ½ cup applesauce for the ½ cup vegetable oil.

INDEX

Notes

Notes

Notes

Notes

CREATIVE COOKING SERIES
for Gift Giving & Flavorful Cooking

GOURMET MUSTARDS: The How-Tos of Making & Cooking with Mustards
HELENE SAWYER AND CHERYL LONG

A must for your pantry! For creative gift-giving and entertaining. Over 125 recipes starring mustard in all its marvelous variety.   ISBN 1-889531-04-9   116 pages $7.95

CLASSIC LIQUEURS: The Art of Making & Cooking with Liqueurs
CHERYL LONG AND HEATHER KIBBEY

Award-winning book showcasing recipes for the famous, hard-to-find and traditional liqueur recipes. Easy instructions yield fabulous results.   ISBN 0-914667-11-4   128 pages $9.95

GOURMET VINEGARS: How to Make & Cook with Them
MARSHA PETERS JOHNSON

Award-winning book reveals in an easy style how to make chef-quality flavored vinegars using fruits, flowers, herbs, spices and veggies. Superb recipes. ISBN 1-889531-05-7 120 pages $6.95

Other intriguing titles from Sibyl Publications:

FOOD NO MATTER WHAT: Stories & Recipes for Perfect Dining in an Imperfect World, LAURA SZABO-COHEN & KARIN KASDIN   ISBN 1-889531-9-4

TAKING CHARGE: Caring Discipline That Works At Home and At School
JOANNE NORDLING, MS, M.ED.   ISBN 1-889531-03-0

SACRED MYTHS: Stories of World Religions, MARILYN McFARLANE   ISBN 0-9638327-7-8

OH BOY OH BOY OH BOY: Confronting Motherhood, Womanhood & Selfhood in a Household of Boys, KARIN KASDIN   ISBN 1-889531-01-4

To Order:
SIBYL Publications • 1007 S.W. Westwood Drive • Portland, OR 97239 • (503) 293-8391 • email: ms@sibylbooks.com

Call 1-800-240-8566

Visit our web site for all of our titles: www.sibylbooks.com